Editorial Project Manager

Eric Migliaccio

Editor in Chief

Karen J. Goldfluss, M.S. Ed.

Cover Artist

Sarah Kim

Illustrator

Clint McKnight

Art Coordinator

Renée Mc Elwee

Imaging

James Edward Grace

Publisher

Mary D. Smith, M.S. Ed.

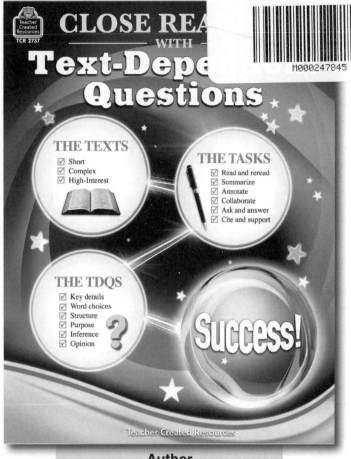

Author

Ruth Foster, M.Ed.

For the Lexile measures of the reading passages included in this book, visit *www.teachercreated.com* and click on the Lexile Measures button located on this resource's product page.

For correlations to the Common Core State Standards, see pages 95–96 of this book or visit *http://www.teachercreated.com/standards.*

Teacher Created Resources, Inc.

12621 Western Avenue

Garden Grove, CA 92841

www.teachercreated.com

ISBN: 978-1-4206-2737-4

© 2017 Teacher Created Resources, Inc.

Made in U.S.A.

Table of Contents

Overview

What Is Close Reading?

Close reading is thoughtful, critical analysis of a text. Close-reading instruction gives your students guided practice in approaching, understanding, and, ultimately, mastering complex texts. This type of instruction builds positive reading habits and allows students to successfully integrate their prior experiences and background knowledge with the unfamiliar text they are encountering.

There are certain factors that differentiate close-reading instruction from other types of reading instruction. These factors include the types of **texts** used for instruction, the **tasks** students are asked to perform, and the **questions** they are expected to answer. For detailed information on these factors, see "A Closer Look" on pages 4–5.

What Are Text-Dependent Questions?

Text-dependent questions (TDQs) can only be answered by referring explicitly back to the text. They are designed to deepen the reader's understanding of the text, and they require students to answer in such a way that higher-level thinking is demonstrated. To be most effective, TDQs should address all that a reading passage has to offer; the questions asked should prompt students to consider the meaning, purpose, structure, and craft contained within the text.

How Is This Guide Organized?

The units in *Close Reading with Text-Dependent Questions* are divided into two sections. Each of the twenty **Section I Units** (pages 8–87) is a four-page unit.

Page 1 **Close-Reading Passage**	This page contains a short, complex, high-interest reading passage. Parts of the passage are numbered for easy reference, and space for annotation is provided in the left margin and between lines of text.
Page 2 **Close-Reading Tasks**	Students are guided to read the passage, summarize it, reread and annotate it, and meet with a partner to discuss and define the author's word choices.
Page 3 **Text-Dependent Questions**	Students are asked to display a general understanding of the text, locate key details within it, cite evidence, and begin to use tools such as inference.
Page 4 **More TDQs**	Students examine the structure of the text and the author's purpose. They form opinions and use evidence to support and defend claims. A research prompt encourages choice, exploration, and cross-curricular connections. (**Note:** Monitor students' Internet research for content appropriateness.)

Each of the two **Section II Units** (pages 88–91) contains two pages.

Page 1 **Close-Reading Passage**	This page contains a short, complex, high-interest reading passage. Parts of the passage are numbered for easy reference, and space for annotation is provided in the left margin and between lines of text.
Page 2 **Peer-Led Tasks**	This page guides groups of students through a series of peer-led tasks in which each member is assigned a different role. Students become teachers to one another as they work together to analyze a text.

A Closer Look

Close Reading with Text-Dependent Questions focuses on the three main components of close-reading instruction: the **texts** students are asked to read, the **tasks** they are instructed to perform, and the **text-dependent questions (TDQs)** they are expected to answer thoughtfully and accurately.

The Texts

- ✓ short
- ✓ complex
- ✓ high-interest
- ✓ multi-genre

Not all texts are appropriate for close-reading instruction. Passages need to be written in a manner that invites analysis and at a level that requires slow, careful, deliberate reading. The texts in this guide achieve these goals in a number of ways.

- **Length:** Close-reading passages should be relatively short because the rigorous work required of students could make longer passages overwhelming.

Each unit in this guide contains a one-page passage of about 325–375 words. This is an ideal length to introduce and explore a subject, while allowing students of this age to conduct an in-depth examination of its content and purpose.

- **Complexity:** The best way to foster close reading of informational or fictional text is through text complexity. Writing achieves a high level of text complexity when it fulfills certain factors. The **purpose** of the text is implicit or hidden in some way, and the **structure** of the text is complex and/or unconventional. The **demands** of the text ask students to use life experiences, cultural awareness, and content knowledge to supplement their understanding. The **language** of the text incorporates domain-specific, figurative, ironic, ambiguous, or otherwise unfamiliar vocabulary.

The passages in this guide contain all of these different types of language and ask students to decipher their meanings in the context of the parts (words, phrases, sentences, etc.) around them. The passages meet the purpose and structure criteria by delaying key information, defying reader expectations, and/or including unexpected outcomes — elements that challenge students to follow the development of ideas along the course of the text. Students must combine their prior knowledge with the information given in order to form and support an opinion.

- **Interest:** Since close reading requires multiple readings, it is vital that the topics covered and style employed be interesting and varied. The passages in this resource will guide your students down such high-interest avenues as adventure, invention, discovery, and oddity. These texts are written with humor and wonder, and they strive to impart the thrill of learning.

- **Text Types and Genres:** It is important to give students experience with the close reading of a wide variety of texts. The passages in this guide are an equal mix of fiction and nonfiction; and they include examples and/or combinations of the following forms, text types, and genres: drama, poetry, descriptive, narrative, expository, and argumentative.

- **Lexile-Leveled:** A Lexile measure is a quantitative tool designed to represent the complexity of a text. The passages featured in this resource have been Lexile-leveled to ensure their appropriateness for this grade level. For more information, visit this resource's product page at *www.teachercreated.com*.

A Closer Look (cont.)

The Tasks

- ✓ read and reread
- ✓ summarize
- ✓ annotate
- ✓ collaborate
- ✓ connect
- ✓ illustrate
- ✓ cite and support
- ✓ ask and answer

An essential way in which close-reading instruction differs from other practices can be seen in the tasks students are asked to perform. This resource focuses on the following student tasks:

- **Read and Reread:** First and foremost, close reading requires multiple readings of the text. This fosters a deeper understanding as the knowledge gained with each successive reading builds upon the previous readings. To keep students engaged, the tasks associated with each reading should vary. When students are asked to reread a passage, they should be given a new purpose or a new group of questions that influences that reading.

- **Annotation:** During at least one reading of the passage, students should annotate, or make notes on, the text. Annotation focuses students' attention on the text and allows them to track their thought processes as they read. It also allows students to interact with the text by noting words, phrases, or ideas that confuse or interest them. When writing about or discussing a text, students can consult their annotations and retrieve valuable information.

> For more information about annotation, see pages 6–7 of this guide.

- **Additional Tasks:** Collaboration allows students to discuss and problem-solve with their partner peers. An emphasis is placed on demonstrating an understanding of unfamiliar words in context and applying academic vocabulary in new ways. Throughout, students are prompted to cite evidence to support claims and reinforce arguments. Often, students are asked to illustrate written information or connect text to visuals. A section of peer-led activities (pages 88–91) encourages students to ask and answer peer-generated questions.

The TDQs

- ✓ general
- ✓ key details
- ✓ word choice
- ✓ sequence
- ✓ structure
- ✓ purpose
- ✓ inference
- ✓ opinion

Text-dependent questions (TDQs) emphasize what the text has to offer as opposed to the students' personal experiences. This helps students focus on the text — from the literal (what it says) to the structural (how it works) to the inferential (what it means).

The TDQs in this resource ask students to demonstrate a wide range of understanding about the text. There is a progression from questions that ask for general understanding to those that require deeper levels of focus. The first question or two are relatively easy to answer, as this promotes student confidence and lessens the possibility for discouragement or disengagement. Subsequent questions delve into increasingly higher-order involvement in the text. Students are asked why a passage is written the way it is and if they feel that the author's choices were ultimately successful. This type of instruction and questioning not only makes students better readers, it also makes them better writers as they consider the decisions authors make and the effects those choices have on the text and the reader.

All About Annotation
Teacher Instructions

Annotation is the practice of making notes on a text during reading, and it is a crucial component of the close-reading process. It allows students to more deeply dissect a text and make note of the parts that intrigue or excite them, as well as the parts that confuse or disengage them. Annotation gives students a tool with which to interact with the text on their terms and in ways specific to their needs and interests.

Tips and Strategies

☑ This resource has been designed to give your students the space needed to annotate the reading passages. Extra space has been included in the margin to the left of the passage. In addition, room has also been added between each line of text, with even more space included between paragraphs.

☑ Share the student sample (page 7) to give your students an idea of what is expected of them and how annotation works. This sample only shows three basic ways of annotating: circling unfamiliar words, underlining main ideas, and writing key details. Begin with these to ensure that students understand the concept. Additional responsibilities and tasks can be added later.

☑ Much like the skill of summarization requires restraint, so does annotation. Give students a goal. For example, tell them they can only underline one main idea per paragraph and/ or their key notes for each paragraph can be no more than five words in length. If these expectations aren't given, students might make too many notes, circle too many words, and underline too much text. This would make the text more difficult to read and create the opposite effect of what is intended.

☑ If you see that a majority of your students are circling the same unfamiliar words and noting confusion in the same areas of the text, spend more time and focus on these parts.

☑ Instruct students to reference their annotations when answering more complex questions, such as those inquiring about the structural and inferential elements of the text.

☑ Annotations can be used as an assessment tool to determine how well students are analyzing a text or even how well they are following directions.

☑ If students need more room to annotate, consider allowing them to affix sticky notes onto their pages and add notes in this way.

☑ As students become more fluent at the skill of annotating, increase their responsibilities and/or add new tasks. Here are a few examples to consider:

   ♦ Add a question mark (?) for information they find confusing.

   ♦ Add an exclamation point (!) for information they find surprising.

   ♦ Draw arrows between ideas and/or elements to show connections.

   ♦ Keep track of characters' names and relationships.

   ♦ Add notes about such elements of authorial craft as tone, mood, or style.

All About Annotation *(cont.)*
Student Sample

Annotation = making notes on a text as you read it

3 Basic Ways to Annotate a Text

Note key details.

In the left margin, write a few words that give key details from the paragraph. Your notes in this space should be brief. They should be five words or fewer.

Circle difficult words.

If you aren't sure what a word means, circle it. Once you determine its meaning, write the word's definition in the left margin and circle it.

Underline main ideas.

Find the main idea of each paragraph and underline it. The main idea gives the most important information the author is trying to tell you in that paragraph.

The Man Who Ate His Beard

hard, solid

dirty beard
ate it

1 Parts of his beard were as hard as wood. The hair had become (solidified) All the fish guts, bird blood, and other gunk in it had turned what was once soft and curly into a solid mass. Using his only knife, the man sawed off part of his beard. He didn't throw it away. He sprinkled it with a few drops of seawater to soften and flavor it. <u>Then he rolled it into a ball and swallowed it.</u> He used some of his precious rainwater to help wash the hairball down.

stuck
somewhere

can't move
can't call
no food

2 On November 17, 2012, Jose Salvador Alvarenga was fishing off the coast of Mexico. <u>A storm struck, and Alvarenga and his companion were left (stranded) and drifting in an open 25-foot boat.</u> They had no oars or engine with which to steer or move the boat. Without a radio, there was no way for them to call for help. They had no food, nor did they have hooks or nets with which to catch any. They had no shelter, only the clothes on their backs.

The Man Who Ate His Beard

Parts of his beard were as hard as wood. The hair had become solidified. All the fish guts, bird blood, and other gunk in it had turned what was once soft and curly into a solid mass. Using his only knife, the man sawed off part of his beard. He didn't throw it away. He sprinkled it with a few drops of seawater to soften and flavor it. Then he rolled it into a ball and swallowed it. He used some of his precious rainwater to help wash the hairball down.

On November 17, 2012, Jose Salvador Alvarenga was fishing off the coast of Mexico. A storm struck, and Alvarenga and his companion were left stranded and drifting in an open 25-foot boat. They had no oars or engine with which to steer or move the boat. Without a radio, there was no way for them to call for help. They had no food, nor did they have hooks or nets with which to catch any. They had no shelter, only the clothes on their backs.

Alvarenga did everything he could to survive. He caught fish, turtles, and birds with his bare hands. He consumed them raw. Wasting nothing, he ate the bones and feathers, too. He drank his own urine and any rainwater he could collect. After several months, Alvarenga's companion refused to eat. Despite Alvarenga's care, his companion died and Alvarenga was on his own.

Alvarenga washed ashore on January 29, 2014. He had landed on a remote and tiny island that was part of the Marshall Islands. Moving so slowly that he became covered in leeches, he crawled inward. He was finally spotted by a women and her husband. They did not know Spanish and had no idea who Alvarenga was.

No one believed Alvarenga to be who he said he was. First, he was 6,700 miles from home! Second, no one had even come close to surviving 438 days at sea stranded in an open boat. Journalists have verified Alvarenga's story. Facts were checked, and scientists studied currents and mapped out his route. As unbelievable as it sounded, it all proved to be true.

Your Name: _____ Partner: _____

The Man Who Ate His Beard (cont.)

First Silently read "The Man Who Ate His Beard." You might see words you do not know and read parts you do not understand. Keep reading! Determine what the story is mainly about.

Then Summarize paragraphs 2–5 only. Write down the main actions and most important information. If someone reads your summary, that person should know it is this story you are writing about, not a different story!

_____

_____

_____

_____

_____

After That Read the story again. Use a pencil to circle or mark words you don't know. Note places that confuse you. Underline the main action or idea of each paragraph.

Next Meet with your partner. Help each other find these words in the text.

> solidified   stranded   drifting   consumed   verified

Read the sentences around the words. Think about how they fit in the whole story. Define the words. Which information from the text helped you and your partner figure out the meaning of the words? An example is given for you.

Word	Definition	Information That Helps
solidified		
stranded	left without the means to move, stuck	"They had no oars or engine with which to steer or move the boat."
drifting		
consumed		
verified		

Your Name: _____

The Man Who Ate His Beard *(cont.)*

Now) Answer the story questions below.

1. Why didn't people believe Alvarenga's story at first? Give two reasons. Use facts from the story in your answer.

_____

_____

_____

2. In what condition were Alvarenga and his companion left after the storm? What things did they have? Quote parts of the story.

_____

_____

_____

Do you think Alvarenga had a stove on the boat? In your answer, quote a sentence from the story to support your claim.

_____

_____

3. What was in Alvarenga's beard? _____

_____

In paragraph 1, the author said parts of Alvarenga's beard were as hard as wood. Why would the author describe it this way?

_____

_____

4. In what condition was Alvarenga when he washed ashore on the island?

_____

How does the author paint this picture? What details help you understand his condition?

_____

_____

_____

Your Name: _____

The Man Who Ate His Beard *(cont.)*

Then   Reread the entire story one last time. Think about how paragraph 1 relates to the rest of the story.

5. Write a very short summary of paragraph 1. What happens in this part of the story?

_____

_____

_____

6. Why do you think the author started the story this way?

_____

_____

_____

In paragraph 1, does the author give you any hints that Alvarenga might be lost at sea? Explain.

_____

_____

_____

7. What if the story ended after the third sentence in paragraph 3? Would you have believed Alvarenga? Why or why not.

_____

_____

_____

Why do you think the author made sure you knew the story was real?

_____

_____

_____

Learn More   Trace Alvarenga's route by finding Mexico, the Pacific Ocean, and the Marshall Islands on a map or globe. If you want, you can find other facts about him and see photos.

Key Search Terms
◆ Alvarenga
◆ 438 days at sea

Andromeda

 "Class," Ms. Marcos said, "Please greet our new student. His name is . . ."

"You can call me 'Andromeda,'" the boy said, suddenly speaking up.
"I won't be here long. I'm only here to observe."

 Ms. Marcos looked startled and opened her mouth to say something, but the boy continued before she could get a word in edgewise. "I'm from the Andromeda galaxy, so calling me 'Andromeda' just makes it easier for all. The Andromeda Galaxy is the nearest major galaxy to yours, the Milky Way Galaxy. We're only 2.5 million light years from each other. My galaxy is shaped like a spiral. The Milky Way is a spiral galaxy, too, but mine is bigger. It measures about 220,000 light years across. The bright central region is visible to the naked eye. From Earth, you can see it on moonless nights, even in areas with moderate light pollution. Of course, it only looks like a star to you because human eyes are so weak."

 "Ms. Marcos looks like she could be knocked over with a feather!" Liam whispered to Olive. Then he said, "Look, he's going to sit next to us!"

 As the boy sat down, Olive smilingly asked him how he got to Earth. When Andromeda answered that he had teleported through a black hole, Liam laughed. "Sure," he scoffed. "You make it sound easy as pie. I don't think so!" Then Liam smiled and said, "Sorry I sounded like I was making fun of you. The truth is that I like your imagination. I have the feeling the three of us are going to have as much fun as a barrel of monkeys."

 When Olive and Liam came to school the next day no one could enter. Firetrucks were in the parking lot. "Don't worry," Ms. Marcos told her students. "No one is hurt. It's just that the building is full of monkeys. No one knows where they came from or how they got there." Liam and Olive went to find Andromeda so they could tell him, but Andromeda hadn't arrived yet. He never did, but there was plenty of pie for lunch.

Your Name: _____   Partner: _____

Andromeda *(cont.)*

First   Silently read "Andromeda." You might see words you do not know and read parts you do not understand. Keep reading! Determine what the story is mainly about.

Then   Summarize paragraphs 1–4 only. Write down the main actions and most important information. If someone reads your summary, that person should know it is this story you are writing about, not a different story!

_____

_____

_____

_____

_____

After That   Read the story again. Use a pencil to circle or mark words you don't know. Note places that confuse you. Underline the main action or idea of each paragraph.

Next   Meet with your partner. Help each other find these words in the text.

     observe   *startled*   *region*   *moderate*   *scoffed*

Read the sentences around the words. Think about what they mean and how they fit in the whole story. Use what you learned to answer the questions below. As you work, check with your partner. Does your partner think your answers make sense?

   a. If I looked at the night sky, I might **observe** _____.

   b. I might be **startled** if a _____ suddenly walked into the room.

   c. My school is in the _____ **region** of the country.
       (For this answer, use a word such as one of the following: Northern, Southern, Eastern, Western, Midwestern.)

   d. One shouldn't have too much _____. A **moderate** amount is best.

   e. I **scoffed** when my friend said _____

       _____.

With your partner, create a new sentence. This sentence should include at least two of these vocabulary words.

_____

_____

Your Name: _____

Andromeda (cont.)

(Now)   Answer the story questions below.

1. Compare and contrast the Andromeda and Milky Way Galaxies.

How are they alike? _____

_____

How are they different? _____

_____

2. Liam tells Olive that Ms. Marcos looks as if she could be "knocked over with a feather." What does this expression mean in the way it is used here?

_____

What parts of the story help you know this?_____

_____

_____

3. What did Ms. Marcos do when Andromeda started talking? Use words and draw a picture to show your answer.

_____

_____

_____

_____

_____

Why didn't Ms. Marco interrupt Andromeda? What words in the story help you know?

_____

_____

4. How did Liam's attitude change in paragraph 4? What words or actions in the story helped you know?

_____

_____

Your Name: _____

Andromeda (cont.)

Then Reread the entire story one last time. Pay attention to how the author makes you feel at the end of the story.

5. In which paragraph does Andromeda first state that he comes from a different galaxy?

Check the box beside your answer. ❏ 1 ❏ 2 ❏ 3 ❏ 4 ❏ 5

In an earlier paragraph, what does he say that foreshadows (hints at) this information.

_____

6. What happens in paragraph 5? Sum it up in a few sentences. _____

_____

_____

Why might this make it seem possible that Andromeda does indeed come from a different galaxy?

_____

_____

7. The author never gives solid proof that Andromeda comes from a different galaxy. She has Liam telling Andromeda that he likes his imagination, but that is before the last paragraph. Do you think this is an effective choice that the author has made? Why or why not?

_____

_____

Write another paragraph to continue the story. Your paragraph should give another hint or two about where Andromeda comes from.

_____

_____

_____

_____

_____

_____

Learn More What does a spiral galaxy look like? What do the three other kinds of galaxies look like? On the back of this paper, draw and label pictures of each.

Weeks Without Stopping

 Frigatebirds are sea birds. They spend most of their lives at sea. The only time they come to land is to raise their chicks. This probably makes you think that these sea birds have waterproof feathers, as ducks, pelicans, and gulls do. Frigatebirds don't! They are sea birds, but they can't swim or land on the water. If they landed on the water, they would drown!

 An ornithologist named Henri Weimerskirch wanted to know more about frigatebirds. He already knew how they fed. Since a frigatebird can't get wet, it gets food two ways. The first way is by stealing food from other birds. It does this by harassing other birds in flight. It doesn't stop pestering until the bird regurgitates (brings back up) fish it has already eaten. The second way happens when they spot a school of smaller fish being chased by larger fish. The smaller fish start leaping out of the water in a wild frenzy, and that's when the frigatebird flies down and scoops them up.

 Weimerskirch wanted to know what the birds did between feeding since they couldn't land on the water. To find out, he put satellite tags and instruments on the birds. This allowed him to locate the birds, track where they were going, and measure things like heart rates.

 One bird flew nonstop for two months! Another bird soared 40 miles over the Indian Ocean without a single wing-flap! All of the birds soared great distances, and they also soared high in the air. Some reached heights over 4,000 meters (about 2.5 miles) above the ocean! It's freezing cold at that altitude, and frigatebirds are tropical birds! They only live where it is warm!

 Weimerskirch found that these birds use little energy. Their heartbeats don't go up. They are efficient fliers in part because of their wingspans. From tip to tip, their wingspans measure six feet. Also, they fly into cumulus clouds. White, fluffy cumulus clouds often form where warm air rises from the surface of the ocean. Once inside the cloud, these birds soar on the updraft. They rise with the warm air all the way to the top of the cloud.

Your Name: _____ Partner: _____

Weeks Without Stopping (cont.)

First Silently read "Weeks Without Stopping." You might see words you do not know and read parts you do not understand. Keep reading! Determine what the story is mainly about.

Then Sum up the story. Write the main actions and most important information. If someone reads your summary, that person should know it is this story you are writing about, not a different story!

_____

_____

_____

_____

_____

_____

After That Read the story again. Use a pencil to circle or mark words you don't know. Note places that confuse you. Underline the main action or idea of each paragraph.

Next Meet with your partner. Help each other find these words in the text.

ornithologist   harassing   regurgitates   frenzy   efficient

Read the sentences around the words. Think about how they fit in the whole story. Think about what the words mean. Explain how the story helps you know the following things:

a. An **ornithologist** does not study insects. _____

_____

b. When you are **harassing** someone, you are bothering them. _____

_____

c. At the moment you **regurgitate** your food, you aren't swallowing it. _____

_____

d. If someone is in a **frenzy**, he/she is not calm and relaxed. The fish are leaping for

their lives. They are the opposite of calm and relaxed.

e. If something runs **efficiently**, it isn't wasting energy. _____

_____

Your Name: _____

Weeks Without Stopping (cont.)

Now   Answer the story questions below.

1. How did Weimerskirch know where the birds went and how often they flapped their wings?

_____

_____

2. How many meters above the ocean did some of the frigatebirds fly? For your answer, use an exact quote from the passage.

_____

_____

Why do the last two sentences of paragraph 4 end with exclamation marks instead of periods? Provide information from the story in your answer.

_____

_____

_____

Do you agree with the author's use of exclamation points in this paragraph? Use information from the story to support your claim.

_____

_____

3. Why do the frigatebirds fly into cumulus clouds and not other kinds of clouds?

_____

_____

_____

4. What is one way the frigatebirds find food?_____

_____

_____

Why do they have to find food this way?_____

_____

_____

Your Name: _____

Weeks Without Stopping *(cont.)*

Then) Reread the entire story one last time. Pay attention to when the title begins to make sense.

5. In what number paragraph are you told about a bird that went "weeks without stopping?"

Check the box beside your answer. ❑ 1 ❑ 2 ❑ 3 ❑ 4 ❑ 5

In what paragraph do you find out why the birds could go weeks without stopping?

Check the box beside your answer. ❑ 1 ❑ 2 ❑ 3 ❑ 4 ❑ 5

6. The author could have titled this story "Frigatebirds." Do you think that would have been a better title? Tell why or why not.

_____

_____

_____

In the box, write a new and different title for the story. Tell why your title is a good title and represents the information given in the story, as well as the style and tone in which it is written.

```
┌─────────────────────────────────┐
│                                 │
│                                 │
│                                 │
└─────────────────────────────────┘
```

_____

_____

_____

7. Imagine someone stole something from you. When caught, the person said, "I can do it, because frigatebirds can." What would you say? Use information from the story.

_____

_____

_____

Learn More) Look in books or online to research how most birds make their feathers waterproof. On the back of this page, write a short paragraph explaining what you learned.

Mysteries Solved

 Ada and Ethan liked mysteries. They wanted to prepare for careers as detectives. Ada and Ethan asked their father for his advice. "Read!" Stephen said. "Read on a variety of subjects, and don't judge a book by its cover." Ada and Ethan didn't really see how reading would help them get jobs as detectives, but they did what their father recommended anyway. They read a lot of books on a lot of different topics.

 Several weeks later, Devon came up to Ada and Ethan in the lunchroom. He said, "Someone wants to sell my dad some gold. My dad is thinking about it, but he isn't sure because it's a lot of money. Do you think he should buy it?" When Ada asked if Devon and his dad had actually seen the gold, Devon said he had. "At first I thought the man didn't bring any because all he was holding was a thin plastic grocery bag. The bag was dangling from his right hand. Then he took out the gold. The man said it was two standard bars. They shone so brightly that it took my breath away."

 Ethan said, "All that glitters is not gold. The man is trying to cheat your father. I once read in a book that a standard bar of gold weighs 12.4 kilograms or just a bit more than 27 pounds. If that man's two bars were real, they would have weighed too much for a thin plastic grocery bag!"

 The next day, a girl came up to Ada and Ethan at recess. "I'm Alice," she said. "Devon said you might help me." When Ethan asked how, Alice said, "My mom saw a painting for sale. It depicted George Washington sitting in the Oval Office at the White House. The art dealer said it was painted during Washington's first term as president. It's expensive, but do you think my mom should buy it? After all, it's a piece of history."

 Ada said, "The art dealer is as crooked as a dog's hind leg. The picture is a fake. I read in a book that George Washington was the only president who didn't live in the White House. He couldn't, because he died before it was built!"

Your Name: _____ Partner: _____

Mysteries Solved *(cont.)*

First Silently read "Mysteries Solved." You might see words you do not know and read parts you do not understand. Keep reading! Determine what the story is mainly about.

Then Sum up the story. Write the main actions and most important information. If someone reads your summary, that person should know it is this story you are writing about.

_____

_____

_____

_____

_____

_____

After That Read the story again. Use a pencil to circle or mark words you don't know. Note places that confuse you. Underline the main action or idea of each paragraph.

Next Meet with your partner. Help each other find these words in the text.

careers   variety   topics   recommended

Read the sentences around the words. Define the words and answer the questions.

a. The word **career** means _____

What career might you want one day? _____

b. The word **topic** means _____

Name a topic that is currently in the news? _____

c. The word **variety** means _____

If you could eat any fruit for breakfast, which would you choose? _____

If you could eat any fruit for dessert, which would you choose? _____

d. The word **recommend** means _____

Which book would you most recommend to your best friend?

_____

Which book would you most recommend to your teacher?

_____

Your Name: _____

Mysteries Solved (cont.)

Now Answer the story questions below.

1. How much does a standard bar of gold weigh? _____

How did knowing this help Ethan know that the man was trying to cheat Devon's father?

_____

_____

2. What two pieces of advice did Ada and Ethan's father give to them? In your answer, use a quotation from the story.

_____

_____

What evidence in the story proves that Ada and Ethan followed their father's advice?

_____

_____

3. Keep track of the cast of fictional characters introduced in this passage. Name five of them. For each, state two facts about the character and note which of the passage's paragraphs the character is named in. One answer is given for you.

Character	Facts	Paragraphs
Ada	sister to Ethan, wants to be a detective	1, 2, 4, 5

4. When Ada says that the art dealer is as "crooked as a dog's hind leg," what does she mean?

_____

Which parts of the story helped you answer?

_____

_____

Your Name: _____

Mysteries Solved *(cont.)*

Then Reread the story one last time. Think about the author's purpose for writing the story.

5. In the first paragraph, what is the main message you are given about reading?

_____

How is that message reinforced in the rest of the story? _____

_____

_____

6. How are the sayings "All that glitters is not gold" and "Don't judge a book by its cover" alike?

_____

_____

Create a cartoon that illustrates one of these sayings <u>as it is used in the passage</u>.

7. Do you think the author did a good job showing the importance of reading? Explain. Use evidence from the story to support your claim.

_____

_____

_____

Can you think of another example or time in your life when reading or having read something helped you know what to do?

_____

_____

Learn More On the back of this paper, write one paragraph on gold or the White House. Find information in books or on the Internet.

The Abominable Snowman

1 When the British reviewed his work, they often criticized him. They didn't like the way he spelled or rhymed. The truth is that the man did take liberties when it came to spelling and rhyming. He once wrote:

If called by a panther / Don't anther.

One may criticize the spelling, but one has to admit that it is very good advice!

2 The man who played around with word spellings and rhymes was Frederic Ogden Nash. A comic writer, Nash wrote over 500 pieces of light verse. The poem "The Abominable Snowman" is an excellent example. In the poem, Nash makes light of something horrible.

I've never seen an abominable snowman, / I'm hoping not to see one,
I'm also hoping, if I do, / That it will be a wee one.

3 In an interview, Nash once said, "I think in terms of rhyme, and have since I was six years old." Despite his way of thinking, Nash said that making rhymes was not always easy. Before Nash was known as a writer of humor, he went to college, but he dropped out after one year. He then worked as a salesman and wrote streetcar card ads.

4 The poem "Song of the Open Road" is humorous. It may have been written to make one laugh, but it has a timely message. It is a gentle reminder of what might happen if we cover the world in signs.

I think that I shall never see / A billboard lovely as a tree.
Indeed, unless the billboards fall / I'll never see a tree at all.

5 Nash spent most of his adult life in Baltimore, Maryland, and thought of the city as his home. The British may not have liked Nash's liberties when it came to spelling, but it is likely that the people of Baltimore didn't mind. After all, it was Nash who wrote, "I could have loved New York had I not loved Balti-more."

Your Name: _____ Partner: _____

The Abominable Snowman *(cont.)*

First Silently read "The Abominable Snowman." You might see words you do not know and read parts you do not understand. Keep reading! Determine what the story is mainly about.

Then Sum up the story. Write the main actions and most important information. If someone reads your summary, that person should know it is this story you are writing about.

_____

_____

_____

_____

_____

_____

After That Read the story again. Use a pencil to circle or mark words you don't know. Note places that confuse you. Underline the main action or idea of each paragraph.

Next Meet with your partner. Help each other find these words in the text.

criticized   liberties   abominable   humorous   timely

Read the sentences around the words. Think about how they fit in the whole story and what the words might mean. Then use what you learn to fill in the blanks.

a. If someone **criticized** a movie, he or she might say _____

_____

b. If someone took away our **liberties**, we might not be able to _____

_____

c. If someone had **abominable** manners, he or she might _____

_____

d. If you saw something **humorous**, you might be seeing _____

_____

e. If you sent someone a **timely** gift, then you may have sent _____

_____

Your Name: _____

The Abominable Snowman *(cont.)*

Now   Answer the story questions below.

1. In paragraph 1, what advice does Nash give? _____

_____

Why is it good advice? _____

_____

_____

Why does he use the word "anther" in paragraph 1? Give two reasons why he uses this word
and spells it this way.

_____

_____

2. According to the story, in what terms does Nash think? _____

_____

Does Nash find it easy to think this way? Defend your answer by rephrasing or quoting some
words from the story.

_____

_____

_____

3. Think about Nash's poem "The Abominable Snowman." If you see something abominable,
why might you hope it is very small?

_____

_____

4. In the story, it says that Nash wrote light verse. What is meant by the phrase "light verse"?

_____

_____

How did the story help you know? _____

_____

_____

Your Name: _____

The Abominable Snowman *(cont.)*

Then　Reread the entire story one last time. Pay attention to when you first learn who the story is about.

5.　Write a very short summary of paragraph 1. In your summary, tell which word was spelled incorrectly.

_____

_____

_____

6.　This passage is titled "The Abominable Snowman." Why might someone criticize this title?

_____

_____

Would the title "Song of the Open Road" be any better? Explain.

_____

_____

7.　Rewrite the title and the first two lines of the first paragraph. Write so that your reader knows sooner what the story is going to be about. (You may use information from other parts of the story in the lines you rewrite.)

_____

_____

_____

Why might some readers like your rewrite better? How might it make a reader read less carefully?

_____

_____

Learn More　Look in books or on the Internet to find examples of more of Nash's verses. Then try your own hand at writing a light verse. Your verse can be one line or longer.

4'33"

1   Mr. and Mrs. Mozart were really worried. The piano recital was coming up in just five days, and they had yet to hear Sally practice for the concert. "She tells me she is practicing," Mr. Mozart said to his wife, "but I don't believe her. If she were telling the truth, we'd be hearing her play."

2   "Maybe she thinks she can be like Glenn Gould," Mrs. Mozart said, trying to reassure her husband. "He often thought about how to play a piece for quite a long time. When he finally sat down to play, he played almost flawlessly. The fingering, the tone, and the rhythm were all perfect."

3   Mr. Mozart wasn't reassured. He meant to talk quietly to Sally about his fears, but when he went into the living room and saw Sally reading a book, he exploded. His voice boiling with rage, he yelled, "Do you think we're made of money? Do you know how much your piano teacher charges us?"

4   Sally answered calmly. She told her father that her recital piece had three movements. She would play each movement perfectly, he would see. The day of the concert, Sally was the last to play. Before sitting down, Sally held up a paper with 4'33" written on it. "I'm playing this piece," she said, "not the one written on the program. You pronounce it 'Four minutes, thirty-three seconds' or just 'Four thirty-three.' It was composed in 1952 by John Cage, an American. The piece contains three movements, or parts."

5   Sally sat down on the piano bench. She closed the keyboard lid. Sometime later she opened it briefly. She did this again two more times. The audience didn't know what to do. They looked at each other with raised eyebrows. When Sally stood up, she had not played a note, but four minutes and thirty-three seconds had passed. The audience may have been shocked, but Sally had played her piece perfectly. "Cage composed this piece so people could hear the sounds around them," she said. "This piece upset a lot of people when he wrote it, and it still does today."

4'33" *(cont.)*

Your Name: _____   Partner: _____

First   Silently read the story. You might see words you do not know and read parts you do not understand. Keep reading! Determine what the story is mainly about.

Then   Sum up the story. Write the main actions and most important information. If someone reads your summary, that person should know it is this story you are writing about.

_____

_____

_____

_____

_____

_____

_____

After That   Read the story again. Use a pencil to circle or mark words you don't know. Note places that confuse you. Underline the main action or idea of each paragraph.

Next   Meet with your partner. Help each other find these words in the text.

       recital   reassure   flawlessly   composed

Read the sentences around the words. Think about how they fit in the whole story. Think about what the words must mean. Decide if each sentence below is **True** or **False**. Tell which information in the story helped you know. The first one is done for you.

   a. A **recital** is the same as a composer. _False. Cage was a composer whose_

    music was played at a recital. A recital is a concert.

   b. When you **reassure** someone, you try to make that person feel better. _____

    _____

    _____

   c. If one sings **flawlessly**, one sings out of tune. _____

    _____

   d. When something is **composed**, it is created or written. _____

    _____

    _____

Your Name: _____

4'33" *(cont.)*

Now   Answer the story questions below.

1. What evidence is there in the story that Sally's teacher did not know what Sally was going to do at the recital?

   _____

   _____

2. How did Sally let the audience know she had started playing and when each movement was over?

   _____

   _____

3. In the last paragraph, it says that the people in the audience looked at each other with "raised eyebrows." What does this expression mean in this sentence?

   _____

   _____

   What happened or what words in the story helped you know this?

   _____

   _____

4. At one point in the story, it says that when Mr. Mozart saw Sally reading a book, he exploded. What exactly does this mean? In the box to the left, draw a picture of what Mr. Mozart must have looked like when this happened. On the lines to the right, explain what the author meant when she used the word "exploded." Use the story to defend your answer.

   _____

   _____

   _____

   _____

   _____

   _____

Your Name: _____

4'33" *(cont.)*

Then) Reread the entire story one last time.

5. Think about the ' and the " in the title of the passage. In mathematical shorthand for time, what do these two marks stand for? Use evidence from the story to defend your answer.

' stands for _____

" stands for _____

Here is how I know this: _____

_____

6. In which paragraph does the title begin to make sense? _____

Why do you think the author made the reader wait to find out what the title meant? If the author had explained what "4'33"" stood for in the first paragraph, how might it have changed the story?

_____

_____

_____

7. Sally said that this piece upsets a lot of people when it is played. Do you think her parents were upset when she played it? Using information from the story, explain why or why not.

_____

_____

_____

Would you be upset if you went to a concert and someone played it? Tell why or why not.

_____

_____

_____

Learn More) Find out more about Mozart, Glenn Gould, or John Cage. Write down five facts about one of them. If you want, you can look on the Internet and see the musical score of "4'33"" or watch it being performed.

> **Key Search Terms**
> ◆ 4'33" *music score*
> ◆ 4'33" *performance*

Flying Through the Eye

1   He was told "bananas." That's the answer meteorologist Bill Evans was given by the pilot who was going to fly him into a hurricane and through its eye. Hurricanes are huge storms. They develop over oceans. They die out over land because they lose their source of moisture. Hurricane winds form a big circle, and they blow in a counterclockwise movement. They can reach speeds over 150 miles per hour. The area inside the circle of winds is called the eye. The air inside the eye is calm. One can see blue skies in the eye.

2   Meteorologists study the atmosphere. They examine the atmosphere's effects on the environment. They predict the weather. They study storms and investigate climate trends.

3   At first, no one thought you could fly into a hurricane. Then in 1943, Joe Duckworth took a dare. Duckworth was a colonel in the U.S. Army. He was helping to train British pilots how to fly with instruments. Before pilots used instruments, they had to look out the window. Instruments made it so pilots could fly at night or when it was too foggy or stormy to see.

4   During the training, a hurricane approached. The British teased the Americans. They said the American planes weren't built well, and they bet that one would fall apart if it were flown into a hurricane. Duckworth flew directly into the storm and into its eye. He won the dare, and he proved that hurricanes could be studied up close.

5   In 1998, Bill Evans was going to fly into a hurricane for his first time. The eye of this hurricane was 22 miles wide. The ride to and from the eye would be extremely rough, with winds blowing at speeds over 160 miles per hour. The plane would violently shake and rattle. Anybody or anything not tightly secured would fly through the cabin. It was common for people to get sick. Before leaving, Evans had asked the pilot what he should have for breakfast. When he was told bananas, Evans asked why. The simple reply was, "Tastes the same coming back up."

Your Name: _____   Partner: _____

Flying Through the Eye (cont.)

First   Silently read "Flying Through the Eye." You might see words you do not know and read parts you do not understand. Keep reading! Determine what the story is mainly about.

Then   Sum up the story. Write the main actions and most important information. If someone reads your summary, that person should know it is this story you are writing about.

_____

_____

_____

_____

_____

After That   Read the story again. Use a pencil to circle or mark words you don't know. Note places that confuse you. Underline the main action or idea of each paragraph.

Next   Meet with your partner. Help each other find these words in the text.

   meteorologist   eye   atmosphere   instruments

Read the sentences around the words. Think about how they fit in the whole story. Think about what the words mean and then answer the questions. Explain how the story helps you know the following things:

a. A **meteorologist** doesn't study dinosaurs. _____

   _____

   _____

b. An **eye** does not have to be something you see with. _____

   _____

   _____

c. Earth's **atmosphere** is not in Earth. It is made up of gases surrounding Earth.

   _____

   _____

d. An **instrument** can refer to something other than a thing used to play music.

   _____

   _____

Your Name: _____

Flying Through the Eye (cont.)

Now   Answer the story questions below.

1. Using information from the story, make a simple drawing of a hurricane. Label the eye and draw an arrow to show what direction the winds are blowing. On the lines to the right, list three details from the story that helped you make your drawing.

———————————————

———————————————

———————————————

———————————————

———————————————

———————————————

2. Indiana is a state in the Midwest. Why is it very rare for Indiana to be struck by a powerful hurricane? Use information from the story to support your answer.

_____

_____

3. According to the story, what happens to a lot of people when they fly into a hurricane?

_____

Why does this happen?

_____

_____

4. In 1943, something happened that led to some British pilots knowing that some American planes were very well built. What happened?

_____

_____

_____

_____

Your Name: _____

Flying Through the Eye *(cont.)*

Then Reread the entire story once more. Notice the information given in each paragraph.

5. The very first sentence of the story is the answer to a question. What is the question?

_____

Where in the story do you find out what the question was? _____

Why do you think the author gave you the answer first? _____

_____

_____

6. Which paragraph is mostly a definition of a word? Check the box beside your answer.

❏ 1 ❏ 2 ❏ 3 ❏ 4 ❏ 5

Why did the author include this paragraph? What does it help you understand about Evans?

_____

_____

_____

7. What do you think might have been Evans's response to what the pilot told him about breakfast? Do you think the pilot's response would make Evans decide not to go on the flight? Use details from the story to support your answer.

_____

_____

_____

Learn More Find out how hurricanes are divided into "categories." Complete the chart below. Then decide which category the hurricane Evans flew into was.

Category	Wind Speeds
1	
2	
3	
4	
5	

The hurricane Evans flew into was likely a Category _____ hurricane. I think this because

_____

_____

_____

The Dig

 Arti (confidently): I just know today is the day. I'm going to find an important artifact. It won't be just some shard of pottery. Nope, no small broken pieces of clay pots for me. I'm going to find something that's intact.

Bali (wistfully): I do wish we could find something all in one piece. I know we're lucky to be here at this dig, but honestly, I never knew archeologists had to work so hard.

 Cici (sternly): We need to stop wasting time talking and get to work.

Arti (teasingly): What's the rush? Archeologists study the past by digging up old things, but trust me, the past isn't going anywhere!

 Bali (excitedly): I've found something! Help me dig it out.

Cici (flabbergasted): I'm shocked! It might be all in one piece!

 Arti (wearily, later in the day): That was a lot of work. I'm exhausted. I've never been so tired. It took hours to dig that thing out, but our being so careful paid off. I'm pretty sure it's intact. Nothing seems to be missing.

Bali (befuddled): It may be all in one piece, but what is it? Two circles connected by a bar? And why does the bar have a T shape at the end?

 Cici (thoughtfully): Do you think you could sit on that thing in the middle of the bar? Could those circles be wheels?

Arti (unbelievingly): Could it be? Is it possible? All that work for a bicycle? Who would want that backward piece of junk? It can't be worth anything!

 LuLu (instructively): As your teacher, let me tell you that someone paid an arm and a leg for that bike when it was new. You can tell by its thin frame and wheels that it was a racing bike. The light frame made it cost more.

Bali (shaking his head): I can't imagine growing up in such an ancient time as the 21st century. Can you imagine having to pedal to get somewhere instead of pushing a button on your flypack?

Your Name: _____ Partner: _____

The Dig (cont.)

First   Silently read "The Dig." You might see words you do not know and read parts you do not understand. Keep reading! Determine what the play is mainly about.

Then   Sum up the play. Write the main actions and most important information. If someone reads your summary, that person should know it is this play you are writing about.

_____

_____

_____

_____

_____

_____

After That   Read the play again. Use a pencil to circle or mark words you don't know. Note places that confuse you. Underline the main action or idea of each paragraph.

Next   Meet with your partner. Look at all the words in the parentheses that describe the character's tone of voice when they are speaking. Use what the characters say to help you define the words. Then take turns choosing one of these words. For each one, write a sentence someone might say when speaking with the same tone of voice. In total, each partner should choose three words to fill out the chart below. The first one is done for you.

Word in Parentheses	What Someone Might Say
confidently	I am sure that I can write great sentences!

Your Name: _____

The Dig (cont.)

Now   Answer the questions below about the play.

1. In which time period do the play's characters live? Check one.

    ❑   the past   ❑   the present   ❑   the future

When in the play do you learn this information? _____

Which character gives you this information, and how does he/she give it?

_____

_____

2. Which of the play's characters explains what archeologists do? _____

What exactly does this person say archeologists do? _____

_____

_____

3. Lulu says that someone "paid an arm and a leg" for the bike. What does this expression mean here?

_____

_____

Which part of the story helps you know that you are right?

_____

_____

4. Most likely, would an archeologist like to find an intact artifact or one that is in shards or fragments? Why? Use information from the story to support your answer.

_____

_____

_____

_____

_____

Your Name: _____

The Dig (cont.)

Then Reread the entire play one last time. Think about how what Bali says at the end changes what you know as you read the play.

5. Tell how knowing what Bali says at the end helps you understand why the characters didn't know the artifact was a bike at first.

_____

_____

Bali describes the artifact as having "a T shape at the end." What is this part he is describing? In the box below, sketch a bicycle. On the lines, answer this question about the T shape.

_____

_____

_____

6. Imagine if this play were to have a narrator. Write a few lines the narrator might say to the audience at the beginning of the play. Your narrator should explain to the audience where and when the play is taking place.

Narrator *(conversationally):* _____

_____

Would having the narrator speak at the beginning of the play make it more or less interesting? Explain.

_____

_____

7. Read the play aloud. Make your voice match the tones in parentheses. Then read the play out loud again, but this time without varying your voices. Which reading was better? Tell why.

_____

_____

Learn More Cities or schools will sometimes make time capsules. The time capsules are buried so that they can be opened in the future. Find out if your school or city has made a time capsule. If so, what was put in it? What would you put in a time capsule? What might archeologists think if they found it 500 years from today? Answer on the back of this paper.

Scurvy Credit

 1 The patient's gums are spongy and swollen. His teeth are loose, and several have fallen out. Wounds fester, and they will not heal. The patient suffers from fatigue. His fatigue is not just when he hasn't had enough sleep. He is tired all the time. His legs hurt, and he bruises easily. There are small red-blue spots all over his skin. The spots are caused by internal bleeding.

 2 The patient is suffering from a disease that is easy to prevent and treat. It must be treated for the patient to live. The disease is scurvy. Before people knew how to prevent scurvy, it was a dreaded disease. Sailors long ago feared it terribly. They would be out at sea for months, and then it would strike the ship. Sailor after sailor would fall ill. Some ships became "ghost ships," as there were not enough men left to crew the ships.

 3 James Lind is given credit for discovering the cure. Lind was a Scottish surgeon in the Royal Navy. By doing experiments, Lind proved that citrus fruit cures scurvy. Lind published his findings in 1753. Oranges, limes, and lemons are all citrus fruits. Lind didn't know why eating citrus fruits prevented scurvy, but today we know why.

 4 Citrus fruits contain vitamin C. So do sweet green peppers, broccoli, and kale. Vitamin C is also known as ascorbic acid. Most animals can synthesize or make their own vitamin C, but humans can't. We must get it from our food. Vitamin C is a water-soluble vitamin. It dissolves in water. This means you must have an ongoing supply in your diet. You can't store it up in your body because any leftover amounts leave your body through urine.

 5 Did Lind really discover the cure? In 1421, a fleet of huge ships set sail from China. They were commanded by a man named Zheng He. The 30,000 men were out at sea for months, but they didn't suffer from scurvy. Every ship carried open tubs in which they planted and sprouted soybeans. Soybeans sprouted in sunlight develop vitamin C. Eaten daily, sprouted soy provides enough vitamin C to prevent scurvy.

Your Name: _____   Partner: _____

Scurvy Credit (cont.)

First   Silently read "Scurvy Credit." You might see words you do not know and read parts you do not understand. Keep reading! Determine what the story is mainly about.

Then   Sum up the story. Write the main actions and most important information. If someone reads your summary, that person should know it is this story you are writing about.

_____

_____

_____

_____

_____

After That   Read the story again. Use a pencil to circle or mark words you don't know. Note places that confuse you. Underline the main action or idea of each paragraph.

Next   Meet with your partner. Help each other find these words in the text.

fester   fatigue   dreaded   credit   soluble

Read the sentences around the words. Think about how they fit in the whole story and what they must mean. Then use what you learned about the words from the story to fill in the blanks. You will use each word one time.

I _____ going on the roller coaster. I told my brother I was too tired

to go. He said, "You can't use _____ as an excuse. I know you're

scared, but I have a pill for you. It will make you brave. Take it with water, and it will melt in your

mouth because it is _____."

The pill worked! It made me brave enough to go on the ride. After the ride, my brother said the

pill was nothing but candy. I was mad! Not wanting my anger to _____,

I decided to tell my brother what I felt right away. Then I thought, "I do have to give my brother

_____ for getting me on this ride! I'm going to go again!"

Your Name: _____

Scurvy Credit *(cont.)*

Now) Answer the story questions below.

1. What are three possible signs of scurvy? _____

_____

_____

_____

2. Are citrus fruits the only foods that contain ascorbic acid? Prove your answer with information from the story.

_____

_____

_____

3. Why is it believed that Zheng He might have known how to prevent scurvy before Lind did?

_____

_____

_____

How exactly did this commander prevent scurvy?

_____

_____

_____

4. Why isn't scurvy a dreaded disease today? _____

_____

_____

What can you do to prevent it and treat it?

_____

_____

Your Name: _____

Scurvy Credit (cont.)

Then Reread the entire story one last time. Pay attention to the information given in each paragraph.

5. Write down the main topic of each paragraph.

Paragraph 1: _____

Paragraph 2: _why scurvy was dreaded_____

Paragraph 3: _____

Paragraph 4: _____

Paragraph 5: _____

6. How did each paragraph having a different topic help you understand the story?

_____

_____

_____

7. In your opinion, can more than one person (or group if they are working together) be given credit for inventing or discovering something? Use information from the story in your answer.

_____

_____

_____

_____

_____

Learn More Investigate! There is one vitamin that is added to milk and other foods, but our bodies will also make it when ultraviolet rays from the sun strike our skin. Which vitamin is it? What would happen to our bones if we don't get enough of this vitamin?

_____

_____

_____

Rat Tale

 Mari's mother said that there were too many flies. Mari's brother suggested that she pay a bounty for each one killed. "The bounty would be an incentive. It would give us a reason to kill them," he said.

 Mari's father said, "I have a rat tale. It's a true story. Before Vietnam was an independent country, it was a colony of France. The French leaders thought there were too many rats in the city of Hanoi. Wanting the rats killed, they set up a bounty program. A person would be paid for every rat tail he or she brought in. The incentive worked. Soon people were bringing in lots of rat tails. The French officials were sure the rat population would decrease. Then they noticed something."

 "What?" Mari and her brother asked. That's when their father told them that the French officials started noticing a lot of rats without tails. People were catching rats and lopping off their tails! Then they were letting the rats go so they could breed and have more rats. The rat population did not decrease. It increased, because people wanted more rat tails. The plan backfired.

 Just then Mari's cousin Rhett came charging in. "You're not going to believe this," he cried, "but I just saw a rat bigger than a cat! I swear it was at least three feet long."

 No one believed Rhett, but that night on the news it was reported that once again there was a threat to the Florida Everglades. The danger was due to a type of rat that was not native to Florida or even the United States. Rats of this type are from Africa. They had been brought to the United States to be sold as pets, but someone had let some go in the Everglades. A city official was quoted as saying, "These rats are Gambian Pouched rats. They can reach three feet in length. We need them killed before they harm the native animals and plants of the Everglades. As an incentive, we will pay a bounty for each tail brought in."

Your Name: _____   Partner: _____

Rat Tale (cont.)

First   Silently read "Rat Tale." You might see words you do not know and read parts you do not understand. Keep reading! Determine what the story is mainly about.

Then   Sum up the story. Write the main actions and most important information. If someone reads your summary, that person should know it is this story you are writing about.

_____

_____

_____

_____

_____

_____

After That   Read the story again. Use a pencil to circle or mark words you don't know. Note places that confuse you. Underline the main action or idea of each paragraph.

Next   Meet with your partner. Help each other find these words in the text.

bounty   incentive   decrease   officials   lopping

Read the sentences around the words. Think about how they fit in the whole story. Define the words. Which information from the text helped you figure out the meaning of the words? An example is given for you.

Word	Definition	Information That Helps
bounty		
incentive	reason, motive for doing something	The bounty was an incentive so people would want to kill rats.
decrease		
officials		
lopping		

Your Name: _____

Rat Tale (cont.)

Now) Answer the story questions below.

1. Why did the French officials offer a bounty for each rat tail? _____

_____

Did the incentive the French offered work? Use evidence from the story in your answer.

_____

_____

_____

2. What was the length of the biggest rats found in Florida? Use the scale provided to draw a rat of that length in the box below. On the lines to the right, quote the part of the story that gave you your answer.

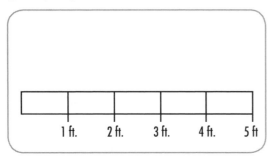

1 ft.   2 ft.   3 ft.   4 ft.   5 ft

_____

_____

_____

3. How did Rhett feel when he saw the rat?

_____

How did the author help you know how Rhett felt?

_____

_____

4. Why were Gambian Pouched rats brought to the United States?

_____

_____

How did they end up in the Florida Everglades?

_____

_____

Your Name: _____

Rat Tale (cont.)

Then) Reread the entire story one last time. Think about the title and the information you are given about rats.

5. What does the word *tale* mean: _____

What does the word *tail* mean: _____

Why might the title of this story be a play on words? _____

_____

_____

6. What might happen to the native animals and plants of the Everglades if a bounty is paid for every Gambian Pouched rat tail? Defend your answer with evidence from the story.

_____

_____

_____

_____

7. What paragraph has nothing in it at all about rats? Check the box beside the correct answer.

❏ 1　　　❏ 2　　　❏ 3　　　❏ 4　　　❏ 5

What purpose does this paragraph have? How does it help the reader understand the remaining paragraphs?

_____

_____

_____

Learn More) Look in books or on the Internet to find out more about the Gambian Pouched rat. Why might its eating habits make it especially harmful in the Everglades? Can you find proof that they are being trained to detect land mines and tuberculosis?

_____

_____

_____

The Big Ear

She had to audition twice. The first time she auditioned at the Royal Academy of Music in London, she was turned down. She was told it was because she was deaf. Evelyn Glennie was indeed deaf. She was born in Scotland in 1965, and she started losing her hearing at the age of eight. By twelve, she was profoundly deaf. She could not hear sounds at all.

The Academy told Glennie that it didn't have a clue as to the future of a deaf musician. Glennie did not feel this was a good reason to be rejected. She insisted she be treated like other students. They were never asked about the future. Instead, they were accepted or rejected due to their ability to perform and to understand and love the art of creating sounds.

Glennie was told she could audition again. This time she was not rejected. She was accepted for all the right reasons. Since then, Glennie has become a world-class musician. She has won many prizes. She is a percussionist. The instruments she plays must be struck or hit. Drums, gongs, and bells are examples of percussion instruments. Cymbals, rattles, or tambourines are other instruments that a percussionist might play.

Glennie lip reads. Lip reading may help her know what people say, but how does she know she is making the correct musical sounds? Glennie often plays with other musicians. She plays in large orchestras. Orchestras have musicians playing all different kinds of instruments. How does Glennie know how to play with the other musicians? How does she know how loud and soft her notes should be?

Glennie says, "I see the body as a big ear." She uses her eyes to see drum skins move as they vibrate. She hears music "through my hands, through my arms, my cheekbones, my skull, my tummy, my chest, my legs, and so on." Glennie often plays barefoot, helping her feel vibrations through her feet. She has become so skillful at feeling vibrations come through her hand that at times she can feel tiny differences with just the tiniest part of her finger.

Your Name: _____ Partner: _____

The Big Ear *(cont.)*

First Silently read "The Big Ear." You might see words you do not know and read parts you do not understand. Keep reading! Determine what the story is mainly about.

Then Sum up the story. Write the main actions and most important information. If someone reads your summary, that person should know it is this story you are writing about.

_____

_____

_____

_____

_____

After That Read the story again. Use a pencil to circle or mark words you don't know. Note places that confuse you. Underline the main action or idea of each paragraph.

Next Meet with your partner. Help each other find these words in the text.

audition   percussionist   rejected   vibration   orchestra

Read the sentences around the words. Think about how they fit in the whole story. Define the words. Which information from the text helped you figure out the meaning of the words? An example is given for you.

Word	Definition	Information That Helps
audition		
percussionist		
rejected		
vibration	movement of something back and forth	Glennie used her eyes to see the drum skins move as they vibrated.
orchestra		

Your Name: _____

The Big Ear *(cont.)*

Now Answer the story questions below.

1. Was Glennie able to hear some sounds at the age of nine? Defend your answer using information from the story.

_____

_____

_____

2. Are the following percussion instruments? For each, check **Yes** or **No**. Use information from the text to support your answer.

violin	guitar	rattle	xylophone
☐ Yes ☐ No	☐ Yes ☐ No	☐ Yes ☐ No	☐ Yes ☐ No

3. You are told that Glennie was accepted for all the right reasons. According to Glennie, what are all the right reasons?

_____

_____

_____

4. Which two senses does Glennie use to "hear"? Explain how she uses them.

Sense #1: _____

_____

Sense #2: _____

_____

Your Name: _____

The Big Ear (cont.)

Then Reread the entire story one last time. Think about if this story is fiction or nonfiction. Think about if it is autobiographical (written by the person whose life is being described) or biographical (written about a person by someone else).

5. Is this story fiction or nonfiction? How can you tell?_____

_____

_____

Is this story autobiographical or biographical? How can you tell?_____

_____

_____

6. Imagine you are Glennie. You have just finished your first audition, and you have been given the news of your rejection. Write a few lines in which you explain what happened and how you feel. As this will be in autographical form, use the pronoun "I" when referring to yourself. Also, be sure to use information you learned from the story.

_____

_____

_____

_____

_____

_____

7. In which paragraph of the story do you find out what instrument Glennie plays?

❏ 1   ❏ 2   ❏ 3   ❏ 4   ❏ 5

Why do you think the author waited until that point to tell you?

_____

_____

_____

Learn More Find out the difference between brass, percussion, stringed, and woodwind instruments. On the back of this paper, write a short paragraph in which you compare them. Give a few examples of each kind of instrument.

Conundrum

 Ms. Enigma told the class to put away their books. She told the class she had a conundrum for them. All the students looked at each other. No one knew what Ms. Enigma meant. Was a conundrum something to eat or watch? Was it something to smell or touch? "It matches my name," Ms. Enigma told the class. "Now listen."

 "A boy is stuck on a deserted island," Ms. Enigma said. "There is a bridge that connects the island to the mainland. A guard stands in the exact middle of the bridge, halfway from the island and the mainland. The guard prohibits anyone from crossing. If you're coming from the mainland, he stops you and sends you back to the mainland. If you're coming from the island, he stops you and sends you back to the island."

 "This same guard," Ms. Enigma continued, "is always present. He sleeps for 30 seconds and then is awake for five minutes. The island is surrounded by man-eating sharks, and there is no other way from the island to the mainland. The boy has nothing but his own shirt and pants. It takes the boy one minute to cross the bridge. He crosses successfully."

 "Now," Ms. Enigma said with a smile, "It is time to solve the conundrum. How did the boy do it?" Puzzled students looked at each other. They were bewildered and felt as if they were drowning in a sea of confusion.

 Then the students solved the puzzle. How the boy did it was no longer an enigma. The students knew that the boy ran up to the guard when he was asleep. The boy then turned around before the guard woke up so when the guard did wake up, it looked as if the boy was running to the island. The guard, believing that the boy came from the mainland, prohibited the boy from returning to the island and made him go to the mainland!

Your Name: _____   Partner: _____

Conundrum (cont.)

First Silently read "Conundrum." You might see words you do not know and read parts you do not understand. Keep reading! Determine what the story is mainly about.

Then Sum up the story. Write the main actions and most important information. If someone reads your summary, that person should know it is this story you are writing about.

_____

_____

_____

_____

_____

_____

After That Read the story again. Use a pencil to circle or mark words you don't know. Note places that confuse you. Underline the main action or idea of each paragraph.

Next Meet with your partner. Help each other find these words in the text.

enigma   conundrum   prohibits   bewildered

Read the sentences around the words to help you figure out what they mean. Then answer the following questions:

a. Which two words are most likely to be synonyms (words that mean almost the same thing)? Check the boxes beside the two words.

❑ enigma   ❑ conundrum   ❑ prohibit   ❑ bewildered

How does the story help you answer this question?   _____

_____

b. Which word is a synonym for "stops" or does "not allow"? _____

How does the story help you answer this question?   _____

_____

c. Which word is a synonym for "confused"? _____

How does the story help you answer this question?   _____

_____

Your Name: _____

Conundrum (cont.)

Now   Answer the story questions below.

1. Why doesn't the boy swim to the mainland? On the lines to the left, quote the sentence or part of the sentence in the story that gives you the answer. In the box to the right, illustrate (draw a picture of) this quote.

   _____

   _____

   _____

2. What two things did the guard have to do in order for the boy to make it successfully across the bridge? Why did he have to do these two things?

   _____

   _____

   _____

   _____

3. In paragraph 4, you are told that the students felt as if they were "drowning in a sea of confusion." What does this expression mean in the way it is used here?

   _____

   _____

   What parts of the story helped you know?

   _____

   _____

4. Would the boy have been able to get to the mainland if it took him 15 minutes to cross the bridge? Use evidence from the story to defend your answer.

   _____

   _____

   _____

Your Name: _____

Conundrum (cont.)

Then Reread the entire story one last time.

5. Think about when the main problem is introduced and when it is solved.

   a. In which two paragraphs are details about the problem given? _____

   b. In which paragraph is the solution to the problem given? _____

   c. Which paragraph serves as an introduction to the problem? _____

   d. Which paragraph serves as a "short rest" or "time to think"? _____

6. Why do you think the author included paragraph 4 in the passage? _____

_____

Did you feel as confused as the students? Tell why or why not. _____

_____

7. Skip the long introduction and story! Rewrite the problem, facts, and solution in the fewest words possible.

   Problem: _____

   Facts: _____

   _____

   Solution: _____

   _____

   Why might some people like the rewrite better than the story? _____

   _____

   _____

   Why might some people like the story better than the rewrite? _____

   _____

   _____

**Learn
More** One famous conundrum is, "What came first, the chicken or the egg?" On the back of this paper, explain in writing why this question is a conundrum. Then, try to think of a riddle or puzzle that you can share with the class.

Small Deer

 Teresa adored folk tales from other countries. She especially liked the stories from Indonesia about Small Deer. Small Deer was very clever. She would often get her way or save herself by tricking other animals. One day, Teresa found a copy of a Small Deer story she had never read before. Teresa curled up in a chair and began to read.

 That night at dinner, Teresa summed up the story for her family. "Small Deer was eating banana leaves and wasn't paying attention to where she was going. She fell into a pit so steep and deep, she couldn't get out. Pig came by and started teasing her because she was trapped. Small Deer told Pig that she wasn't trapped. She had jumped in on purpose because the world was going to end, and the pit was the only safe place to be. That made Pig want to jump in, but Small Deer said he couldn't because anyone who sneezed had to be thrown out of the pit, and Pig sneezed too much.

 "Pig begged and pleaded. He promised he wouldn't sneeze, and finally Small Deer relented and said he could jump into the pit. The same thing happened when Elephant and Tiger came by. Teasing would turn to pleading, and finally, Small Deer would relent and allow them to jump in. Each was given several warnings: anyone who sneezed would be thrown out of the pit."

 Teresa took a deep breath before continuing with her narration. "Small Deer made a big show of trying to not sneeze. Then of course, she did. Despite her protests, the other animals threw her out of the pit. Once out, she went off to eat more banana leaves in peace." There was silence for a moment while Teresa's family thought about the story Teresa had just recounted.

 "That's a story to knock your socks off," Teresa's brother, Nick, said. "It's fascinating because I think Small Deer is a bit like Anansi, the tricky spider in some African folk tales." Suddenly, Nick sneezed a thundering sneeze. After he sneezed, Nick said, "You can make me leave if you want." Nick was told that his trick wouldn't work. He had to stay and help clear the table.

Your Name: _____   Partner: _____

Small Deer *(cont.)*

First   Silently read "Small Deer." You might see words you do not know and read parts you do not understand. Keep reading! Determine what the story is mainly about.

Then   Sum up <u>only the parts about Small Deer</u>. Write down the main actions and most important information. If someone reads your summary, that person should know it is this story you are writing about.

_____

_____

_____

_____

_____

After That   Read the story again. Use a pencil to circle or mark words you don't know. Note places that confuse you. Underline the main action or idea of each paragraph.

Next   Meet with your partner. Help each other find these words in the text.

adored   pleaded   relented   narration   recounted

Read the sentences around the words. You and your partner should think about how the words fit in the whole story and what they might mean. Then circle **True** or **False** for each statement below. On the line below each statement, use information from the story to tell why your answers are correct.

a. If something is **adored**, it is disliked.   **True**   **False**

    How you know: _____

b. If you **plead** for something, you beg for it.   **True**   **False**

    How you know: _____

c. If you **relent**, you give in.   **True**   **False**

    How you know: _____

d. If you **narrate** something, you listen to it.   **True**   **False**

    How you know: _____

e. If you **recount** something, you must count numbers.   **True**   **False**

    How you know: _____

Your Name: _____

Small Deer (cont.)

Now   Answer the story questions below.

1. How many different kinds of animals were in the pit with Small Deer? _____

What kind were they? In the box below, draw and label (give the name of) each one.

2. Do you think Small Deer had a plan for getting out as soon as Pig talked to her? Tell why or why not.

_____

_____

3. Nick used the expression "to knock your socks off." What did he mean?

_____

_____

How do you know this is what he meant? Which parts of the story helped you know?

_____

_____

_____

4. Are folk tales only told in Indonesia? Use two pieces of evidence from the story to support your answer.

_____

_____

_____

Your Name: _____

Small Deer (cont.)

Then — Reread the entire story one last time. Think about how there was a story within a story.

5. Sum up the first and last paragraphs only.

_____

_____

_____

_____

6. What was the last thing Nick said in the story? Quote his words exactly.

_____

Would his words have made any sense if there had not been a story (tale) within a story?

_____

_____

_____

7. Why might an author put a story within a story?

_____

_____

_____

If the author had only written about Small Deer, how would the story have started? Write one or two lines of a possible story start.

_____

_____

_____

_____

Learn More — Find another story about Small Deer (sometimes called Mouse Deer) or Anansi in books or online. On the back of this paper, recount the story in your own words.

Mother, May I?

1 "Mother, may I? Mother, may I?" Mrs. Timber didn't take her eyes from her phone. Her fingers were a blur of motion as she tapped the screen. She snapped at Fabian for him to leave her alone, but he was persistent. He was not going to give up. "Mother, may I?" he asked again and again.

2 "Yes!" Mrs. Timber cried out, the irritation she felt coming out in her tone of voice. It wasn't until much later that Mrs. Timber stopped to wonder what she had said yes to. She wasn't irritated when she found out. She felt quite the opposite, in fact. "My son is wonderful," she happily told her friend Tilda. "He says he is going to build a kite so he can fly around the world, but he wanted my permission first."

3 Two days later, Fabian was still at it. Mrs. Timber came to inspect his progress. When she commented that it was bigger than she had expected, Fabian told her it couldn't be any smaller. "It couldn't lift you," he told his mother, "but it's perfect for me."

4 "He's so cute," Mrs. Timber bragged to her friend as the two sat drinking coffee and eating cookies. "He told me he will take off from the peak of Frisco Hill. He says at that elevation and running full speed a strong gust of wind will be enough to get him airborne." When her friend pointed out that the top of Frisco Hill really wasn't that high, Mrs. Timber shrugged. "Of course, he's going to fail," she said, cramming the last cookie into her mouth. "But he's been so intent on building his kite that he hasn't pestered me in two days. I'll be sad when it's finished."

5 That evening Fabian announced he was ready for his trip around the world. Mrs. Timber went with him to Frisco Hill. Intent on her phone screen, she ignored him, even as Fabian began to run. When Mrs. Timber looked up, Fabian was soaring high above the treetops. While she stood open-mouthed and rooted to the ground, Fabian's words were carried to her on the wind. "Mother, I can!"

Your Name: _____ Partner: _____

Mother, May I? (cont.)

First   Silently read "Mother, May I?" You might see words you do not know and read parts you do not understand. Keep reading! Determine what the story is mainly about.

Then   Sum up the story. Write the main actions and most important information. If someone reads your summary, that person should know it is this story you are writing about.

_____

_____

_____

_____

_____

_____

After That   Read the story again. Use a pencil to circle or mark words you don't know. Note places that confuse you. Underline the main action or idea of each paragraph.

Next   Meet with your partner. Help each other find these words in the text.

     persistent   irritation   peak   elevation   gust

Read the sentences around the words. Think about how they fit in the whole story. Define the words. Which information from the text helped you and your partner figure out the meaning of the words? An example is given for you.

Word	Definition	Information That Helps
persistent		
irritation	frustration, annoyance, the state of being bothered	Mrs. Timber was happy when she wasn't being irritated by Fabian asking if he may.
peak		
elevation		
gust		

Your Name: _____

Mother, May I? *(cont.)*

(Now)   Answer the story questions below.

1. What did Fabian need to become airborne? Name three things.

_____

_____

_____

2. Why was Mrs. Timber pleased that Fabian was building a kite?

_____

_____

How do you know Mrs. Timber didn't expect Fabian to succeed? Quote some of Mrs. Timber's exact words in your answer.

_____

_____

_____

3. In the last paragraph, you are told that Mrs. Timber is "rooted to the ground." What does this expression mean here?

_____

_____

How do you know you are right? Tell which part of the story helped you know.

_____

_____

_____

4. Use evidence from the story to show that Mrs. Timber was using her phone too much.

_____

_____

_____

Your Name: _____

Mother, May I? *(cont.)*

Then Reread the entire story one last time. As you read, think about how this story compares to fairy tales you have read.

5. Fairy tales are often written so that there is a good character and an evil character. Could this story be considered a modern fairy tale? Explain.

_____

_____

_____

6. Paragraph 4 contains these two sentences:

♦ Mrs. Timber bragged to her friend as the two sat drinking coffee and eating cookies.

♦ "Of course he's going to fail," she said, cramming the last cookie into her mouth.

Do these two sentences help to paint a positive or negative image of Mrs. Timber? Explain. Which words from those sentences most help paint this image of Mrs. Timber?

_____

_____

_____

7. Rewrite the two sentences quoted from paragraph 4 in such a way that Mrs. Timber comes across as the opposite of how she is presented now.

_____

_____

_____

_____

Do your new sentences make the story better or worse? Tell why you think so.

_____

_____

Learn More Who invented the first kites? Find out by reading in books or conducting online research. Find out four other kite facts, too. On the back of this paper, write an informative paragraph to share what you learned.

Selling Time

1   In 1892, Ruth Belville started to sell time. Belville was successful at selling time. Her customers trusted her. They were pleased with her service. Reliable and punctual, she never let her customers down. Summer or winter, she never missed a delivery or was ever late. Belville continued to sell time until 1940. She was in her eighties, but she didn't retire because of her age. She retired only when the Second World War made it impossible to continue walking along the streets safely.

2   Why would anyone sell time? Perhaps the better question is why would anyone buy time? Today it is easy to get the correct time. New technology has made it possible. We can hear the time on the radio. We can check our phones. We can look on our computers. Our phones and computer do not need to be reset. They will automatically adjust to the time zone they are in.

3   In 1836, none of these new technologies were available. Clockmakers needed to know the correct time. How else could they know if their clocks were correct? Other business people needed the correct time, too. How else could they know when to meet or talk to people? John Belville was Ruth's father. He was an astronomer at the Royal Observatory Greenwich. He was the one who started to sell the correct time. After his death, his wife took the business over. Then his daughter Ruth did. All three of them used the same watch. They would set it every morning to the time in the observatory.

4   The world is divided into east and west. The line that divides the world is man-made. It is at 0 degrees longitude. It is called the prime meridian, and it runs through Greenwich, England. Time is measured at this line. Clocks and time zones are set by Greenwich Meridian Time.

5   The watch the Belville family used was a pocket watch. It was state of the art. There was nothing better. It was very accurate. It provided time to an accuracy of a tenth of a second. Time may have been delivered once a week and by horse and buggy, but it was time worth paying for.

Your Name: _____ Partner: _____

Selling Time *(cont.)*

First Silently read "Selling Time." You might see words you do not know and read parts you do not understand. Keep reading! Determine what the story is mainly about.

Then Sum up the story. Write the main actions and most important information. If someone reads your summary, that person should know it is this story you are writing about.

_____

_____

_____

_____

_____

_____

After That Read the story again. Use a pencil to circle or mark words you don't know. Note places that confuse you. Underline the main action or idea of each paragraph.

Next Meet with your partner. Help each other find these words in the text.

reliable   punctual   accurate

Read the sentences around the words. Think about how they fit in the whole story. Discuss how the author helped you know what the words meant. Then pick one word each. Fill in the blanks.

a. My partner's word: _____

My partner thinks that in this passage the word must mean _____

_____

I agree, because in the passage _____

_____

b. My word: _____

I think that in this passage this word must mean _____

_____

My partner agrees, because in the passage _____

_____

Your Name: _____

Selling Time (cont.)

(Now) Answer the story questions below.

1. Why did Ruth Belville stop selling time? _____

_____

_____

2. What made it possible for the Belville family to be able to sell time? Explain using two pieces of evidence from the story.

_____

_____

_____

How accurate was the Belville family pocket watch? Use a quotation to show your answer.

_____

_____

3. In the last paragraph, the pocket watch is described as "state of the art." Tell what this expression means by using information from the story.

_____

_____

Do you think the pocket watch would still be described as "state of the art"? Why or why not?

_____

_____

Name something that you think would still be described as "state of the art". Explain why it could be called this.

_____

_____

4. Why might one think that Ruth Belville liked selling time? Support your answer with evidence from the story.

_____

_____

_____

Your Name: _____

Selling Time (cont.)

Then   Reread the entire story once more. Think about how paragraph 4 fits into the story.

5. Is "Ruth Belville" or "selling time" mentioned in paragraph 4? _____

In one or two sentences, tell what paragraph 4 is mainly about.

_____

_____

_____

6. Why do you think the author included paragraph 4?

_____

_____

_____

Do you think this paragraph helped you understand why Ruth Belville was able to sell time? Tell why or why not.

_____

_____

7. What might happen at your school if everyone had different times on their clocks and phones? Give a general statement, and then think up a specific example.

_____

_____

_____

Learn More   Use a globe or map to locate the Prime Meridian. Find out what your longitude is, and if you are in the Eastern or Western Hemisphere. Look at a map of time zones, too. See how each time zone adds or subtracts hours from Greenwich Meridian Time (GMT).

Key Search Terms	◆ Prime Meridian
	◆ GMT
	◆ hemispheres
	◆ world time zone map

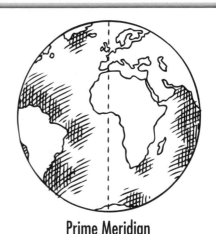

Prime Meridian

Ludicrous Records

1 Records are important. It is serious business when it comes to things like who runs the fastest or who can jump the highest. It is also nice to know what animal has the biggest eyes or the biggest ears. (A squid found in 2008 had eyes bigger than a dinner plate, and no animal has ears larger than the African elephant.)

2 Some world records, however, are ludicrous. They are simply ridiculous. They are trivial and not important. For example, there is a record for most clothespins clipped onto one's face. This silly record was set on July 17, 2013. On that day, Garry Turner clipped 161 clothespins onto his face.

3 It is absurd to think that anyone would care how many balloons a person could inflate with his nose in an hour. One may wonder why anyone would be so foolish as to try! Yet on March 3, 2013, a man named Ashrita Furman inflated balloons with his nose. His record of blowing up 380 still stands today. Furman also holds the record for pushing an orange with his nose. It took 22 minutes and 41 seconds for Furman to push the orange one mile.

4 Other world records go beyond silly. They border on disgusting.   For example, some people don't cut their fingernails. One woman's fingernails grew to a total of 28 feet and 4.5 inches long! How could she get anything done? Could she really keep them clean? One man had ear hair that measured 7.12 inches long. One wonders why he didn't just snip it off.

5 The jury is still out when it comes to some records. For example, there is the case of Mischo Erban. Erban went faster than the highway speed limit. He went over 80 miles per hour. This was on a road. Erban wasn't in a car. He was standing on his skateboard! Is racing downhill on a skateboard any more outlandish or strange than skiing downhill on snow? You have to be strong for both sports. You have to have great balance. You run the risk of great harm.

Your Name: _____   Partner: _____

Ludicrous Records (cont.)

First Silently read "Ludicrous Records." You might see words you do not know and read parts you do not understand. Keep reading! Determine what the story is mainly about.

Then Sum up the story. Write the main actions and most important information. If someone reads your summary, that person should know it is this story you are writing about.

_____

_____

_____

_____

_____

_____

After That Read the story again. Use a pencil to circle or mark words you don't know. Note places that confuse you. Underline the main action or idea of each paragraph.

Next Meet with your partner. Help each other find these words in the text.

ludicrous   trivial   absurd   inflated   outlandish

Read the sentences around the words. Think about how they fit in the whole story. Think about what the words might mean. Then answer **T** (True) or **F** (False). Using information from the story, tell why the false answers are not true. The first one is done for you.

___F___ **a.** If something is **trivial**, it is important. In the story, it says that if something is

trivial, it is not important.

_____ **b.** If something is **ludicrous**, it is silly or ridiculous. _____

_____

_____ **c.** If something is **absurd**, it is foolish or silly. _____

_____

_____ **d.** If something is **inflated**, it is made smaller. _____

_____

_____ **e.** If something is **outlandish**, it is usual and normal. _____

_____

Your Name: _____

Ludicrous Records *(cont.)*

Now   Answer the story questions below.

1. Which two records does the author say border on disgusting? _____

_____

2. How did Furman move the orange? On the lines, describe the answer. In the box, draw it.

_____

_____

_____

_____

Do you think the author was impressed with Furman's orange record? Tell why or why not.

_____

_____

3. In the last paragraph, the author writes that "the jury is still out" when it comes to some records. What is meant by this expression?

_____

_____

Which parts of the story help you know?

_____

_____

4. The deepest SCUBA dive was 1,090 feet in the Red Sea. The fastest shark is the shortfin mako shark. It can go 60 miles per hour. Most likely, would the author think these records are serious or ludicrous? Quote the two sentences from the story that help you defend your answer the most.

_____

_____

_____

_____

_____

Your Name: _____

Ludicrous Records *(cont.)*

Then   Reread the entire story once more. Decide if the author is expressing an opinion or not.

5. Is this story fiction or nonfiction? How do you know? _____

_____

6. Does the author express an opinion? If she does, what is it? _____

_____

Does the reader have to agree with the author? Explain._____

_____

Do you agree with the author? Why or why not? _____

_____

_____

_____

7. How does the title help you understand the author's opinion?

_____

_____

_____

At what point in the story does the reader begin to understand how the title relates to the author's opinion? Check the box beside the paragraph in which this happens. Then explain.

❏   1   ❏   2   ❏   3   ❏   4   ❏   5

_____

_____

_____

_____

Learn More   Research one or two world records. What was the event? Who holds the record? Did the current world record break a previous world record?

I Didn't Even Want It

1   Have you ever received a gift that you wished you had never gotten? Perhaps you opened up a beautifully wrapped box only to find a pair of pea-green tights. Perhaps you excitedly opened up a fancy gift bag only to find a toy more appropriate for a baby — a rattle, for example. Even if you didn't want the gift, there is still something you do.

2   You write a thank-you note. You do this to be polite and courteous, but the note is more than that. It shows gift givers that you think they are special. They are worth your time.

3   The start of a thank-you note is usually an easy step. You just have to make sure that you have used the correct form and spelling of the person's name. One also has to put a comma after the name. "Dear Aunt Michele and Uncle Barack," and "Dear Dr. Ifeelsick," are good examples.

4   Immediately after the greeting, you should express your thanks. You could start with "Thank you so much for . . ." or "I was so happy . . ." To make sure the person knows the note is just for them, add one or two details. For example, "The shirt you gave me is my favorite color," or "I'm going to put the money toward the bike I've been saving for."

5   Of course, you're going to end your note with a "Sincerely," "Yours truly," "Many thanks," or "With love," but what two things do you do before that? You write a bit about the future, and you restate your thanks. In regards to the future, you might write, "I look forward to seeing you soon" or "Can't wait to use your gift immediately!" When you restate your thanks, say "thank you" in a slightly different way than how you said it before. You can do this by adding a new detail. Examples of this would be, "Once again, thanks for the paint set. It has the perfect number of colors," or "I thank you again for the umbrella. Just looking at it makes me wish for rain!"

Your Name: _____ Partner: _____

I Didn't Even Want It *(cont.)*

First Silently read "I Didn't Even Want It." You might see words you do not know and read parts you do not understand. Keep reading! Determine what the story is mainly about.

Then Sum up the story. Write the main actions and most important information. If someone reads your summary, that person should know it is this story you are writing about.

_____

_____

_____

_____

_____

_____

After That Read the story again. Use a pencil to circle or mark words you don't know. Note places that confuse you. Underline the main action or idea of each paragraph.

Next Meet with your partner. Help each other find these words in the text.

      received   *appropriate*   *courteous*   *express*

Read the sentences around the words. Think about how they fit in the whole story. Discuss how the author helped you know what the words meant. Then pick one word each. Fill in the blanks.

a. My partner's word: _____

    My partner thinks that in this passage the word must mean _____

    _____

    I agree because in the passage, _____

    _____

b. My word: _____

    I think that in this passage this word must mean _____

    _____

    My partner agrees because in the passage, _____

    _____

Your Name: _____

I Didn't Even Want It (cont.)

Now — Answer the story questions below.

1. Why does one write a thank-you note? _____

_____

What does it show someone? _____

_____

_____

2. How do the words "pea-green" help you picture exactly what color the tights are?

_____

Would you have the same picture in your mind if the tights were lime-green or forest-green? Explain.

_____

_____

3. Do you think the author thinks pea-green tights are beautiful? Using evidence from the story, tell why or why not.

_____

_____

_____

4. Look at the following thank-you note greeting. It contains mistakes. Rewrite it correctly in the blank box to the right. Use your best or fanciest handwriting.

deer grindpa.

What words in the story tell you that the greeting on the left is not proper or correct?

_____

_____

_____

Your Name: _____

I Didn't Even Want It (cont.)

Then | Reread the entire story one last time. Pay attention to how the first two paragraphs differ from the last three paragraphs.

5. Why might the first two paragraphs be called the introduction of a how-to?

_____

_____

_____

6. The last three paragraphs contain five steps for writing a thank-you note. List the steps in order. Give a brief example for each step.

_____

_____

_____

_____

_____

7. Did the title help you know you were going to learn how to write a thank-you note? Explain.

_____

_____

What might be a better title for this story? _____

_____

Explain your choice. _____

_____

_____

Learn More | Imagine an ornithologist or ichthyologist comes to speak to your class. On a separate piece of paper, write a thank-you note to one of them. You will have to find out what an ornithologist or ichthyologist does so you can include a detail about something they might have told you.

Shooting Stars

 1 "Look at that!" Cooper pointed in excitement up at the night sky. "I just saw a shooting star, so now I can make a wish."

 2 Taylor shook her head and said, "Wishing is wasting time. You have to act, and technically, what you saw wasn't a shooting star. You saw a meteor. A meteoroid is a piece of interplanetary matter that is smaller than a kilometer. When meteoroids enter Earth's atmosphere, they burn up. Technically, a meteor is the flash of light that we see as the meteoroid burns up as it is passing through Earth's atmosphere. Most meteoroids are so small that they vaporize and burn up completely before they reach Earth's surface. If any piece does get to the Earth's surface, it is no longer a meteoroid. Technically, it is now a meteorite. Most meteorites are really small, but once in a blue moon one the size of a 200-pound boulder comes crashing down."

 3 Cooper looked at his friend. "You really know how to spoil the mood," he said. "I know that wishing doesn't work. I know you have to work to make wishes come true. It's just that my mom is really down on her luck right now. My wishing that her luck would change was just my way of showing that I was thinking about her."

 4 Taylor patted Cooper on the back. "That's a good thing to wish for. I'll tell you what. Let's sit here until we see another meteor, and I'll wish for the same thing." The two friends sat looking up at the night sky. They didn't see one more meteor. They saw seven! With each flash of light, Cooper and Taylor wished good fortune on Cooper's mother.

 5 Suddenly, a strange scream cut through the darkness. Cooper and Taylor raced into Cooper's house. They found Cooper's mother clutching her phone, tears streaming down her face. Seeing their worried expressions, Cooper's mother quickly smiled and explained. "I'm only crying because I'm so happy. All that work I put into going back to school has paid off. I've just been offered a new job, the very one I was wishing for!"

Your Name: _____   Partner: _____

Shooting Stars (cont.)

First Silently read "Shooting Stars." You might see words you do not know and read parts you do not understand. Keep reading! Determine what the story is mainly about.

Then Sum up the story. Write the main actions and most important information. If someone reads your summary, that person should know it is this story you are writing about.

_____
_____
_____
_____
_____
_____
_____
_____

**After
That** Read the story again. Use a pencil to circle or mark words you don't know. Note places that confuse you. Underline the main action or idea of each paragraph.

Next Meet with your partner. Help each other find these words in the text.

meteor   meteoroid   meteorite

Read the sentences around the words. Think about how the words are tied together but how they all mean a different thing. Together, use the words to answer the questions below. Your answer should be in the form of a question.

a. I am a piece of interplanetary matter that has landed on Earth's surface.

_____

b. I am a flash of light that is seen when a piece of interplanetary matter is burning up in Earth's atmosphere.

_____

c. I am a piece of interplanetary matter that has entered Earth's atmosphere but has not yet landed on Earth's surface.

_____

Your Name: _____

Shooting Stars *(cont.)*

Now   Answer the story questions below.

1. Most likely, what was Cooper's mom feeling when she screamed? _____

_____

Use evidence from the story to defend your answer. _____

_____

_____

2. According to Taylor's description, which would you be the least likely to see with your own eyes: a meteor, a meteoroid, or a meteorite? Check the box beside your choice and then use information from the story to defend your answer.

❑ meteor   ❑ meteoroid   ❑ meteorite

_____

_____

_____

_____

3. In paragraph 2, Taylor uses the expression "once in a blue moon." What does she mean?

_____

How did the words and the structure of the sentence help you know? _____

_____

_____

4. What does Taylor think about making wishes? _____

_____

_____

Why does she make seven wishes? _____

_____

Your Name: _____

Shooting Stars (cont.)

Then) Reread the entire story one last time. Pay attention to how the second paragraph differs from all the others.

5. What is paragraph 2 mainly about?_____

_____

In what way(s) does it differ from the other paragraphs? _____

_____

_____

6. Imagine if most of the second paragraph were not included. Reread the story one more time, but this time only read the first three sentences of the second paragraph before moving on to the third paragraph.

   a. In this new version, what would be the last word of the paragraph 2? _____

   b. Do you like this new, shorter version of the story better than the original (longer) version? Explain.

   _____

   _____

   c. Why do you think the author put so much information in the second paragraph?

   _____

   _____

7. Do you think Taylor was a good friend to Cooper? Tell why or why not. Use examples from the story.

_____

_____

_____

Learn More) Think about why scientists feel one of the best places to find meteorites is in Antarctica. Then look in books or online to find out if you were correct.

Key Search Terms
◆ finding meteorites
◆ Antarctica

Vomit Safe

1   "I don't care if they do it to defend themselves," Lizzy said to Ramon. "Vomiting is disgusting. It's just not right. They have wings. Why don't they just fly away? That's what I'd do."

2   Ramon laughed and said, "Birds may have wings, but they can't fly when they're little chicks. You're looking at it from the wrong perspective. Change your view. You see it as disgusting, but you should instead think of it as amazing. You've got a tiny fulmar chick perched on a seaside cliff. The bird looks helpless, but it's safe from any predator that creeps up to the nest or swoops down on it. That's because the chick does more than vomit. It does projectile vomiting!"

3   Ramon knew Lizzy didn't understand what projectile vomiting was because of the bewildered look on her face. "I'll explain," Ramon said. "Projectile vomiting is when the vomit is used as a projectile. Fulmar chicks aim and shoot. What comes out is this oily, stinky mess. The stench is horrible. It's a rotten fish smell, and it won't come off, even if you scrub for hours. It's sticky too, so any attacking bird gets its feathers glued together. This makes it hard for the predator bird to fly, and if it tries to swim away, it drowns."

4   Lizzy thought about what she had just learned. "I guess I have to learn to accept our differences," she said slowly. "It's hard to think of projectile vomiting as a good thing, but not everyone can be like us. I have to view the world through others' eyes."

5   Just then something grabbed Lizzy from the back! She struggled with all her might, but she felt herself being lifted into the air. When it seemed that there was no escape, her tail came off. While Lizzy and Ramon darted under a rock to safety, Lizzy's tail wriggled and jerked. "Autotomy is so much better than projectile vomiting," Lizzy said. "My tail will grow back, and once it's safe, we can go eat my old one. What a fat feast we two lizards will have!"

Your Name: _____   Partner: _____

Vomit Safe *(cont.)*

First   Silently read "Vomit Safe." You might see words you do not know and read parts you do not understand. Keep reading! Determine what the story is mainly about.

Then   Sum up the story. Write the main actions and most important information. If someone reads your summary, that person should know it is this story you are writing about.

_____

_____

_____

_____

_____

_____

After That   Read the story again. Use a pencil to circle or mark words you don't know. Note places that confuse you. Underline the main action or idea of each paragraph.

Next   Meet with your partner. Help each other find these words in the text.

   perspective   projectile   bewildered   stench   autotomy

Read the sentences around the words. Think about how they fit in the whole story. Then choose three of the questions below to answer. Use information from the story.

   a. Why might you think a shoe was enormous if you were looking at it from an ant's **perspective**?

   _____

   b. Which is more likely to be a **projectile**, a rocket or a house? Why?

   _____

   c. Why might you feel **bewildered** if someone spoke to you in a foreign language?

   _____

   d. Why might someone say a skunk's defense is its **stench**?

   _____

   e. Why might a predator be surprised if an animal defends itself with **autotomy**?

   _____

Your Name: _____

Vomit Safe (cont.)

Now   Answer the story questions below.

1. How does Lizzy's perspective on vomiting change? _____

_____

_____

2. How does vomiting differ from projectile vomiting? _____

_____

_____

Why is projectile vomiting a better form of defense than just vomiting? _____

_____

_____

_____

3. Why do you think projectile vomiting is a better defense for fulmar chicks than autotomy? (**Hint:** Think about what Lizzy and Ramon do after Lizzy's tail falls off.)

_____

_____

_____

_____

4. What is fulmar vomit like? Quote at least three phrases from the story in your answer.

_____

_____

_____

What is it about the vomit that makes it so birds can't fly or swim? _____

_____

_____

Your Name: _____

Vomit Safe (cont.)

Then)   Reread the entire story once more. Think about what the big lesson of the story might be.

5. The story teaches a life lesson that is summed up in paragraph 4. What is the lesson?

_____

_____

_____

_____

6. When do you find out that Lizzy and Ramon are lizards? Check the box beside the paragraph.

❑ 1   ❑ 2   ❑ 3   ❑ 4   ❑ 5

Why do you think the writer waited until this point before letting you know?

_____

_____

_____

_____

7. What is your first reaction when you hear about something eating a part of its own body?

_____

_____

_____

_____

Change your perspective, and think like a lizard. Why might a lizard want to eat its tail?

_____

_____

_____

_____

Learn More)   Find out five facts about fulmars, or find out about lizards that defends themselves with autonomy. Write down your facts in paragraph form. Use the back of this paper.

The Price

 Lily and Sam were walking along the shore on a sizzling hot summer day. Lily told Sam that the heat had made her thirsty, and she needed a drink to quench her thirst. The two friends walked up to a vending machine with bottled water. "A bottle costs a dollar," Lily said. "I know, because I bought one from this same vending machine yesterday."

 Lily was wrong. One bottle cost two dollars! "I wonder," Sam said, "if this is one of those new vending machines with the adjustable prices." Seeing Lily's puzzled expression, Sam explained that some vending machines were being made so that the price of the product changed according to the temperature. "When it's sizzling hot like today," Sam continued, "people are more likely to be willing to pay more."

 Lily was indignant. "That makes me really angry," she said. "I'm as mad as a hornet, because that's just plain unfair. The price should be the same so that everyone pays the same. That's the way it's always been before, and that's the way it should stay."

 Sam explained that it hadn't always been that way. For many years, prices were never the same! People had to bargain every time they went shopping. There were a few exceptions. For example, some Quaker merchants didn't haggle. They gave everyone the same price. They did this out of their belief that all men are equal before God.

 Lily was surprised when Sam said it was a man named John Wanamaker who made price tags common. He had several department stores. In 1861, he started using price tags. They were attached to his products in a way that they were easily seen. Other venders started doing the same, and today it is a common practice all around the world. Sam said that having price tags also meant that one could hire salespeople more easily. The salespeople no longer had to haggle. This meant they didn't have to know what every item in the store was worth. They could just quote the price on the tag.

Your Name: _____   Partner: _____

The Price *(cont.)*

First Silently read "The Price." You might see words you do not know and read parts you do not understand. Keep reading! Determine what the story is mainly about.

Then Sum up the story. Write the main actions and most important information. If someone reads your summary, that person should know it is this story you are writing about.

_____

_____

_____

_____

_____

After That Read the story again. Use a pencil to circle or mark words you don't know. Note places that confuse you. Underline the main action or idea of each paragraph.

Next Meet with your partner. Help each other find these words in the text.

    sizzling   quench   vending   indignant   haggle

Read the sentences around the words. Think about how they fit in the whole story. Define the words. Which information from the text helped you and your partner figure out the meaning of the words? An example is given for you.

Word	Definition	Information That Helps
sizzling		
quench		
vending	selling	Lily goes to buy water from a vending machine, and other venders started using price tags.
indignant		
haggle		

Your Name: _____

The Price (cont.)

Now   Answer the story questions below.

1. Why might someone pay less or more than another person before 1861?

_____

_____

What happened in 1861 to change this? Your answer should give some details from the story.

_____

_____

_____

2. Most likely, what was the temperature like the day Lily bought a bottle of water for one dollar?

_____

Use information from the story to defend your answer.

_____

_____

_____

3. In paragraph 3, Lily says that she is "as mad as a hornet." What does she mean by this?

_____

Tell which parts of the story helped you answer.

_____

_____

4. Before 1861, why would a salesperson in Wanamaker's store have to know the price of every item in the store in order to haggle with a customer?

_____

_____

Your Name: _____

The Price (cont.)

Then Reread the entire story one last time. Pay attention to how true facts are part of the story.

5. Is this story fiction or nonfiction? _____

How do you know? _____

_____

_____

6. Read paragraphs 4 and 5, but start each paragraph at its second line. If these were the only parts of the story someone read, why might the reader think the story is nonfiction?

_____

_____

_____

_____

7. Imagine you are writing a nonfiction paper on price tags. Write the first two lines of your paper. Think about which information you would begin with.

_____

_____

_____

_____

How do your lines differ in tone than the first two lines of "The Price"?

_____

_____

Learn More Compare the prices of several of the same items (for example, two different brands of the same type of food). You can do this by going into stores, reading ads, or looking up items online. On the back of this paper, tell why you think the prices differ, why someone might buy something that isn't the cheapest price, and why some stores sell some items at below cost.

Man Against Horse

 1
Could modern horses go 100 miles in a day? The 100 miles to be covered was not on a smooth track. They were on a rugged trail in California from Lake Tahoe to Auburn. To prove that horses were capable of such a feat, a race was held in 1955. Contestants had to complete the ride in 24 hours or less. When they crossed the finish line, their mounts had to be judged "fit to continue."

 2
The race proved so popular that it has become an annual event. A man named Gordy Ainsleigh competed in and completed this endurance race in 1971 and 1972. Ainsleigh had to pull out at the 29-mile checkpoint in 1973 because his horse came up lame. In 1974, Ainsleigh decided he would enter the race on foot. It would be man against horse.

 3
Whether human or equine, completing the course is a true test of endurance. There is the 100-mile distance, and there is the rugged trail. The trail winds up and down. In some places, it is very steep. It goes a total of 18,090 feet (5,514 m) up. The cumulative total for the downhill is 22,970 feet (7,000 m). It can be very cold in the highest passes. Contestants often have to go through snow. In contrast, down in the valleys near the end of the course, temperatures can be hot and sweltering.

 4
How did Ainsleigh do? Did he prove that man can compete against horse? He did! It took him 23 hours and 42 minutes. Other people wanted to do what Ainsleigh did. Today, there are two endurance races. There is the Western States Trail Ride for horses. Then there is the Western States Endurance Run for people.

 5
The running race is limited to fewer than 400 people. Many more wish they could enter. Top runners from other races are invited. For the rest, there is a lottery. If they are lucky, their names are chosen. One man ran the race 25 times! All of his times were under 24 hours. In 2012, another man won with a time of 14 hours, 46 minutes, and 44 seconds!

Your Name: _____

Man Against Horse (cont.)

For this activity, work in groups of four. If your group has fewer than four members, share the Mr./Ms. Future task. Begin by deciding who will perform each task.

Title	Student's Name	What Is Your Task?
Mr./Ms. Meaning		Explain the meanings of unfamiliar words.
Mr./Ms. Plot		Summarize what is happening in the passage.
Mr./Ms. Ask		Ask important questions about the passage.
Mr./Ms. Future		Guess what will happen next in the passage.

(First) Read paragraphs 1–2 of "Man Against Horse." Then stop and do the following:

Mr./Ms. Meaning: Define these words for your group: *rugged, capable, feat,* and *endurance.*

Mr./Ms. Plot: Summarize what happened in paragraphs 1–2. Tell how knowing what *rugged, capable, feat,* and *endurance* mean helps you know what is going on.

Mr./Ms. Ask: Check to see if your group knows what is going on by asking a question about the race and Ainsleigh.

Mr./Ms. Future: Guess what is going to happen next. Who do you think is going to win the race?

(Next) Read paragraphs 1–4 of "Man Against Horse." Then stop and do the following:

Mr./Ms. Meaning: Define these words for your group: *equine, cumulative,* and *sweltering.*

Mr./Ms. Plot: Remind the group what happened in paragraphs 1–2. Then sum up for your group what happened in paragraphs 3–4.

Mr./Ms. Ask: Ask a what/where/why/how question (one each) about Ainsleigh and the race.

Mr./Ms. Future: Think about how far 100 miles is, how rugged the trail is, and how fast people can run it. Do you think other runners have beaten Ainsleigh's time?

(Then) Read the entire passage from start to finish. As a group, do the following:

- Discuss the ending of the story. Share what you think! Are you surprised so many people want to run in the race? Why do you think the number of contestants is limited? Do you think it is easier to beat a record than set a record for the first time?
- Find and share quotes from the passage that help you understand how difficult the race is.
- Talk about the author's purpose in writing this story. Do you think the author wanted you to think people were better than horses? Do you think the author wanted you to start thinking about what you might achieve one day? Share your opinions with the group.
- Take a vote: Would each of you rather be in the horse race or the running race?

(Finally) On a separate piece of paper, write a short summary of your group's discussion.

Liar, Liar

1   Merit couldn't wait for the evening's festivities. There was going to be a fancy dinner, and afterward, an oratory contest. The winner of the speech contest would be the one who told the biggest lie! "You've got to come," Merit told her friend Brianna. "How often is one rewarded for lying?"

2   Terry spoke first. Confident and poised, he spoke clearly and without any sign of nervousness. "I saved my money so I could get a new bike. At first, I thought I had bought a lemon. Two hours after I got it, the front wheel began to rattle. I looked to make sure things were all right. That's when I saw a little chain hanging from inside the fender. I pulled on the chain, and the next thing I knew I was spinning around and around. I was like a human top! I spun so fast that I had to wait for time to catch up with me."

3   After Terry, it was Julia's turn to stretch the truth. "Terry says he went fast," Julia said, "but I went faster. Last night I got up to turn off the light. I was back in bed before it got dark!"

4   Andrew stood when it was his turn and said, "It's been so hot here lately that I had to ship in ice from the North Pole. I put it in the chicken coop to help cool the hen's water. I know it worked, because my hens are no longer laying hard-boiled eggs."

5   After Andrew spoke, Brianna slowly stood up. Merit was astonished, because Brianna was ordinarily shy and reluctant to do anything that brought attention to her. Brianna cleared her throat nervously, but when she spoke, Merit knew without a doubt who was the top liar. "I'm sorry," Brianna said, her voice trembling, "but it seems I've come on the wrong night. I thought tonight was a liar's night. I've heard nothing but the truth."

Your Name: _____

Liar, Liar (cont.)

For this activity, work in groups of four. If your group has fewer than four members, share the Mr./Ms. Future task. Begin by deciding who will perform each task.

Title	Student's Name	What Is Your Task?
Mr./Ms. Meaning		Explain the meanings of unfamiliar words.
Mr./Ms. Plot		Summarize what is happening in the passage.
Mr./Ms. Ask		Ask important questions about the passage.
Mr./Ms. Future		Guess what will happen next in the passage.

First   Read paragraphs 1–2 of "Liar, Liar." Then stop reading and do the following:

Mr./Ms. Meaning: What do the words *festivities, oratory, poised,* and *top* mean? Tell your group.

Mr./Ms. Plot: Summarize what happened in paragraphs 1–2. Tell how knowing what *festivities, oratory, poised,* and *top* mean helps you know what is going on.

Mr./Ms. Ask: Check to see if your group knows what is going on by asking a question about the contest and Terry.

Mr./Ms. Future: Guess what is going to happen next. Do you think Terry is going to win the contest? Do you think Merit will tell a lie?

Next   Read paragraphs 1–4 of "Liar, Liar." Then stop reading and do the following:

Mr./Ms. Meaning: Think about what the phrases "bought a lemon" (paragraph 2) and "stretch the truth" (paragraph 3) mean. Tell your group what you think.

Mr./Ms. Plot: Remind the group what happened in paragraphs 1–2. Then sum up for your group what happened in paragraphs 3–4.

Mr./Ms. Ask: Ask one what/where/why/how/who question about each speaker.

Mr./Ms. Future: Who do you think will win the contest? Why?

Then   Read the entire passage from start to finish. As a group, do the following:

♦ Discuss the ending of the story. Share what you think! Who told the biggest lie? Why?

♦ Find and share some quotes from the passage that help you understand why Merit was astonished when Brianna spoke.

♦ What was the author's purpose in writing this story? Does the author want you to believe any of the characters? Does she approve of lying? Share your opinions with the group.

♦ Each one of you should say something that "bends the truth." Whose lie was the funniest? Whose lie was the most believable?

Finally   On a separate piece of paper, write a short summary of your group's discussion.

"The Man Who Ate His Beard" (pages 8–11)

Summary: A man was lost at sea for 438 days. He ate what he could catch with his bare hands. His companion died. The man finally reached land and survived.

Vocabulary: solidified = "turned to a solid"; *drifting* = "carried slowly by current or air"; *consumed* = "ate"; *verified* = "checked to be true"

1. He had drifted over 6,700 miles, and no one had survived 438 days stranded at sea before.
2. They were "stranded and drifting," "without a radio," "had no food or hooks or nets," "no shelter, only the clothes on their backs"; no, because "He consumed them raw."
3. fish guts and blood and other gunk; so the reader understands just how hard and tough it has gotten.
4. He was very weak; he crawled and moved so slowly that leeches stuck to him.
5. A man's beard is so dirty it has turned hard. He cuts off pieces and eats them.
6. In paragraph 1, the author mentions fish guts, bird blood, and sea water.

"Andromeda" (pages 12–15)

Summary: A new boy tells a class he is from the Andromeda Galaxy and gives facts about it. Students joke with him and use the phrases "easy as pie" and "as much fun as a barrel of monkeys."

1. *Alike:* both spiral galaxies; *Different:* Andromeda bigger, Earth not part of it.
2. She is really surprised. We are told that she is startled at what the boy first says, and she must feel even more so after he says he is from another galaxy.
3. She looked startled and opened her mouth to say something; Andromeda continued talking before "she could get a word in edgewise."
4. He was a bit mean at first, because he laughed and scoffed. He apologized and said that he liked the boy's imagination and that they would have fun together.
5. Paragraph 2. In paragraph 1, he says he's here to observe and won't be long.
6. The next day, students can't go inside the school because somehow monkeys have been let loose in there. There is also pie. Andromeda is not there.

"Weeks Without Stopping" (pages 16–19)

Summary: Some sea birds can't land on the water because their feathers aren't waterproof. They steal food or eat leaping fish. They can soar for weeks.

Vocabulary: a. *ornithologist* = "scientist who studies birds"; b. *harassing* = "pestering"; c. *regurgitate* = "bring back up"; e. *efficiently* = "with little wasted energy"

1. He put satellite tags and instruments on the birds that provided the information.
2. "Some reached heights over 4,000 meters above the ocean!"; they are tropical birds and live only where it is warm, but at that altitude it is freezing cold.
3. Cumulus clouds form where warm air is rising from the ocean surface, and the birds want to soar up on the warm air.
4. They harass other birds into throwing up food, and they scoop up fish leaping out of water. Their feathers aren't waterproof, so they could drown.
5. paragraph 4; paragraph 5

"Mysteries Solved" (pages 20–23)

Summary: Ada and Ethan solve two mysteries by using what they learned when they read books. One mystery is about gold, and the other is about George Washington.

Vocabulary: career = "job, profession"; *topic* = "subject"; *variety* = "a mixture of different types"; *recommend* = "to suggest"

1. 12.4 kilograms (about 27 pounds); two bars are too heavy for a plastic bag.
2. He said, "Read on a variety of subjects, and don't judge a book by its cover"; they said that they got the information from reading books.

3. *Ada:* sister, wants to be detective, reads books; 1, 2, 4, 5. *Ethan:* brother, wants to be detective, reads books; 1, 2, 3, 4. *Stephen:* father, reading is important; 1; *Devon:* boy in school lunchroom, asks about buying gold; 2; *Alice:* girl at recess, asks about buying painting; 4.
4. She means that the art dealer is not being truthful, which is proven by the next sentences, in which she proves that the picture is a fake.
5. You should read a lot and read all kinds of books; Ada and Ethan were able to answer the questions because they had read on two very different subjects.
6. They both mean that you can't judge something only by appearance.

"The Abominable Snowman" (pages 24–27)

Summary: Ogden Nash wrote over 500 pieces of light verse. Some were critical of his spelling and rhyming, but Nash's poems made people laugh and made good sense.

1. Do not answer if a panther calls; a panther is a wild cat, and going near it could put you in danger; "anther" sounds like "answer" and rhymes with "panther."
2. He thinks in terms of rhyme; no, because it says that Nash says that, "making rhymes was not always easy."
3. It would be less frightening and easier to deal with.
4. Light verse is humorous or funny. It is not to be taken too seriously; you are told that Nash wrote light verse, and the examples you are given are all humorous.
5. The British don't like someone because of his liberties with spelling and rhyming. For example, he wrote "anther" for "answer."
6. This title is misleading, because the passage is not about an abominable snowman. This other title has the same problem as the first one.

"4'33"" (pages 28–31)

Summary: Sally's parents don't think she is practicing for her recital, but Sally surprises everyone by playing a piece that contains no notes!

Vocabulary: reassure: True; *flawlessly:* False; *composed:* True

1. Sally said that she was going to play a different piece than the one that was written in the program.
2. To start, she put the keyboard lid down. She opened it and closed it at the end of each movement.
3. Everyone was surprised and not really sure what to think. We read that the audience "didn't know what to do."
4. It means that Mr. Mozart got really angry and showed it.
5. The single mark stands for minutes, while the double stands for seconds; Sally's paper reads "4'33"" and she says "four minutes and thirty-three seconds."
6. paragraph 4
7. Yes, Mr. Mozart wanted Sally to practice and yelled about how much they were paying the teacher. One doesn't need to have a teacher to play this piece.

"Flying Through the Eye" (pages 32–35)

Summary: The story is about a meteorologist who flew through a hurricane. Hurricanes have circular winds and an eye. One was first flown into in 1943.

Vocabulary: meteorologist = "one who studies the atmosphere"; *eye* = "area inside a hurricane"; *atmosphere* = "area above Earth"; *instrument* = "gauge used to fly plane"

1. Student diagrams should show a circular storm blowing in a counterclockwise direction. There should be a calm (or blank) spot in the middle where the eye is.
2. Indiana is not close to an ocean. As they travel over land, hurricanes lose their source of moisture and die out.
3. They get sick (throw up); the plane violently shakes and rattles and everything unsecured flies through the cabin.
4. They bet the Americans that one would fall apart if it was flown into a hurricane. A man named Duckworth then flew one into a hurricane, and it didn't fall apart.

5. What should someone have for breakfast before flying into a hurricane; we find out the answer at the end of the last paragraph.

6. paragraph 2; this shows us why a meteorologist would need to fly into hurricane and that Evans is doing this because it is his job to do so.

"The Dig" (pages 36–39)

Summary: At an archeological dig, some people find a bicycle, but at first they don't know what it is. The people are from a future time when bicycles are no longer used.

1. the future; at the very end of the play; Bali; refers to the 21st century as ancient.

2. Arti; he says, "Archeologists study the past by digging up old things."

3. It was very expensive; LuLu says the bike cost a lot because of its light frame.

4. An intact artifact would be better, because it is whole and it would be easier to determine what it is or comes from.

5. They are from the future, where flypacks are the main way to get around. To them, the 21st century is an ancient time. The "bar with a T" = handlebars.

"Scurvy Credit" (pages 40–43)

Summary: The symptoms of scurvy and how to prevent it are described. Credit is given to James Lind, but a commander sprouted soybeans on his ships long before.

Vocabulary: dreaded; fatigue; soluble; fester; credit

1. Possible answers: gums spongy and swollen, loose teeth or falling out, fatigue, legs hurt, bruises, red-blue spots on skin

2. No, because in the story we are told that ascorbic acid is Vitamin C and that sweet green peppers, broccoli, and kale contain Vitamin C.

3. He was out at sea for months, but his men didn't suffer from scurvy; every ship carried open tubs in which to plant and sprout soybeans for the crew to eat.

4. We know that Vitamin C, which is easily available, can cure it. To treat or prevent it, one can eat citrus fruits, broccoli, kale, or even soybeans.

5. 1: symptoms of scurvy; 2: why scurvy was dreaded; 3: James Lind and the cure for scurvy; 4: vitamin C information; 5: how Zheng He prevented scurvy

"Rat Tale" (pages 44–47)

Summary: A story is told about a bounty meant to decrease the rat population and how it backfired. Huge rats are discovered. A bounty is being offered for their tails.

Vocabulary: *bounty* = "reward or price paid for something"; *decrease* = "go down, lessen"; *officials* = "people in charge, officers"; *lopping* = "cutting off, chopping"

1. They wanted people to kill the rats so the rat population would go down.

2. No, because people started lopping off the rat tails and letting them go so the rats would breed more rats.

3. He felt excited and anxious to tell others, he wasn't sure if they would believe him; he came "charging in," and he cried out the news.

4. They had been brought to the United States to be sold as pets; someone let them go in the Everglades.

5. *tale* = "story"; *tail* = "end of an animal"; the story is a tale about rat tails.

6. They might be harmed because the rat population might increase if people start cutting off rat tails and releasing the rats so they can breed.

7. paragraph 1; it acts as an introduction and makes sure the reader knows what a bounty and incentive are.

"The Big Ear" (pages 48–51)

Summary: A deaf woman has become a world-class percussionist. She uses her whole body as a big ear and has trained herself to use every part of her body to "hear" music.

Vocabulary: *audition* = "try out"; *percussionist* = "musician who plays instruments that must be struck or hit"; *rejected* = "turned down"; *orchestra* = "many musicians playing different instruments together"

1. Yes, she wasn't profoundly deaf until 12.

2. *no:* violin or guitar; you do not hit these instruments; *yes:* rattle (shaken, causing parts inside to strike the sides) and xylophone (struck with sticks).

3. having the ability to perform and to understand and love the creation of sounds

4. *sight:* lip reads so knows what people say, looks at drum skins vibrating; *touch:* feels vibrations through feet or other body parts

5. *nonfiction:* It describes a real person and facts about her life; *biographical:* no first-person narrative, when Glennie's words are spoken, they are quoted.

7. paragraph 3; might make reader wonder what kind of instrument she could play

"Conundrum" (pages 52–55)

Summary: A teacher gives her class a conundrum that they solve. The puzzle deals with how a boy goes from an island to the mainland across a bridge with a guard.

Vocabulary: a. *enigma* and *conundrum;* b. *prohibit;* c. *bewildered*

1. "The island is surrounded by man-eating sharks."

2. He had to fall asleep and had to send people back to where they came from; if the guard never fell asleep, he would know where the boy was coming from.

3. They were very confused, puzzled, or bewildered.

4. No, because he would not have gotten halfway across before the guard woke up and saw where he was coming from.

5. a. 2 and 3; b. 5; c. 1; d. 4

6. gives readers time to wonder about the problem and try to think of a solution

7. *problem:* boy on island, wants to get to mainland; *facts:* only way across is bridge, sharks in water, takes 1 minute to cross bridge, guard halfway on bridge sleeps 30 seconds and then awake for 5 minutes, lets no one pass and sends anyone back; *solution:* boy runs to sleeping guard and turns around so it looks as if came from mainland, guard sends boy "back" to mainland.

"Small Deer" (pages 56–59)

Summary: Small Deer is a character from Indonesian folk tales. Small Deer falls into a pit and tricks other animals into jumping inside and then throwing her out.

Vocabulary: a. False; b. True; c. True; d. False; e. False

1. four: Small Deer, Pig, Tiger, and Elephant

2. Yes, because she told Pig he would be thrown out if he sneezed, and then she was the one who sneezed once there were enough animals to throw her out.

3. He meant that the story was great and surprising.

4. No, because we are told that "Teresa adored folk tales from other countries" and that Small Deer is similar to a character from African folk tales.

5. Teresa likes to read Indonesian folk tales, and she reads one about Small Deer. Her brother says he likes the Small Deer tale and tries to use the same trick.

6. "You can make me leave if you want." No, because you wouldn't have known that Small Deer used a sneeze to get out of something.

"Mother, May I?" (pages 60–63)

Summary: A boy asks to make a kite and fly around the world. His mother is distracted by her phone and doesn't pay attention to him. She is shocked when he does it.

Vocabulary: *persistent* = "keeping to something, not giving up"; *peak* = "top"; *elevation* = "height"; *gust* = "strong blast of wind"

1. He needed to be at an elevation at least as high as Frisco Hill, to run full speed, and to have a strong gust of wind.

2. He was so busy working on his kite that he hadn't pestered her for two days; She said, "Of course, he's going to fail."

3. She is so surprised, she can't move. She is shocked that Fabian is flying because she expected the kite to fail, and she is open-mouthed.

4. She said yes to her son when she didn't even know what he was asking. She doesn't see him take off at the end.

5. Yes, because it is fantasy. The mom is the evil character who cares more about her phone than her son. The son is the good character who gets to escape.

6. They paint a negative image. They make her sound as if she is showing off and eating with bad manners.

"Selling Time" (pages 64–67)
Summary: Ruth Belville sold time to watchmakers and business people. She set her watch to Greenwich Meridian Time, and then she told the time to people who paid her.

Vocabulary: reliable = "trustworthy, never letting someone down"; *punctual* = "on time"; *accurate* = "correct"

1. The Second World War made it impossible to continue walking the streets safely.

2. They had an accurate pocket watch, and they could check the time at the Greenwich Observatory; "It provided time to an accuracy of a tenth of a second."

3. It means the watch was the newest and best up to date possible; no, because new technologies have been developed.

4. She didn't retire until she was in her eighties and then only for safety reasons.

5. no; Greenwich Meridian Time is explained, as well as the man-made prime meridian line at 0 degrees longitude.

6. It explains how time is set around the world.

"Ludicrous Records" (pages 68–71)
Summary: While some records are important, the author thinks others are not. She gives examples of ones she thinks are silly, unnecessary, and/or disgusting.

Vocabulary: a. False, not important; b.True; c. True; d. False, bigger; e. False, strange

1. the longest fingernails and the longest ear hair

2. He moved it with his nose; no, because she writes about it in the same paragraph where she calls his other record absurd and calls him foolish to try.

3. She means she has not yet decided if those records are worthwhile or silly.

4. She would think they are serious; she writes that it "is serious business when it comes to things like who runs the fastest or who can jump the highest."

5. It is nonfiction. The author puts in real facts and events.

6. Yes. She feels that some records are serious, others ludicrous, and others are disgusting; the reader does not have to agree or disagree.

7. It tells the reader plainly that some records are silly; paragraph 2, when the reader find out what the word *ludicrous* means.

"I Didn't Even Want It" (pages 72–75)
Summary: Thank-you notes are an important part of receiving gifts. There are some simple steps to follow when writing thank-you notes.

Vocabulary: received = "got something"; *appropriate* = "fit or correct"; *courteous* = "polite, well-mannered"; *express* = "say, state"

1. One gives a note to be polite and courteous; thank-you notes show someone that he/she is special and worth your time.

2. There are many shades of green. By describing the tights as pea-green, the author tells us exactly what shade the tights are.

3. No, because the author writes, "Perhaps you opened up a beautifully wrapped box only to find a pair of pea-green tights." The words "only to find" are a sign that the author doesn't think this would be a good thing to find.

4. "Dear Grandpa," (capitalized and spelled correctly with a comma at the end)

5. They don't tell you how to write a thank-you note, just why you should.

6. Step 1: Use a greeting; Step 2: Express thanks; Step 3: Write a bit about the future; Step 4: Restate your thanks; Step 5: Write an ending.

"Shooting Stars" (pages 76–79)
Summary: Two friends look at the stars. One wishes on a shooting star, and the other explains what a shooting star really is. The wish comes true as a result of hard work.

Vocabulary: a. What is a meteorite?; b. What is a meteor?; c. What is a meteoroid?

1. She was feeling happy and excited, and perhaps surprised and proud; she said she was crying because she was so happy, and she had just gotten a new job.

2. meteoroid; it is interplanetary matter that has entered Earth's atmosphere but hasn't landed; a meteor is a flash of light, and a meteorite can be on the ground.

3. It means "not often, very rarely"; the expression comes after the word *but*, which means that it has to be different from most.

4. She says, "Wishing is wasting time"; she is a good friend to Cooper, and she wants him to know that she is thinking about him and his mom.

5. It's about the difference between a meteor, meteoroid, and meteorite. It gives an explanation of scientific facts, not about the story of these two characters.

6. a. "meteor"

"Vomit Safe" (pages 80–83)
Summary: Lizzy is disgusted by chicks that vomit to defend themselves. She learns about perspective. It turns out that she is a lizard who defends herself by losing her tail.

1. At first she thinks it is disgusting, but then she understands that it is for defense.

2. Vomiting means that your vomit just comes out. With projectile vomiting, it shoots out, and it can be controlled and directed at predators.

3. Fulmar chicks are stuck on the cliff edge. They can't run away and hide, so they need the predator to leave.

4. It is an "oily, stinky mess." It has a "stench that is horrible." "It won't come off." "It's sticky." With glued-together wings, a bird can't fly or swim.

5. We must learn to accept our differences and see the world through others' eyes.

6. paragraph 5

"The Price" (pages 84–87)
Summary: Lily and Sam discuss prices and price tags after they find that the cost of water has gone up. Before price tags started in 1861, people had to haggle.

Vocabulary: sizzling = "really hot"; *quench* = "satisfy"; *indignant* = "angry, irritated"; *haggle* = "to bargain"

1. Prices weren't set, so everyone had to bargain. In 1861, a man named John Wanamaker started using price tags in his department stores.

2. Most likely, it was cooler the day before; Sam says that the vending machine adjusts the price according to the temperature; the bottle cost less on that day.

3. She is very angry; it says in the story that she's indignant and feels it is unfair.

4. The salesperson would not want to agree on a price that was too low and cost less than what the store owner had to pay for the item.

5. It is fiction; it's about two friends, and nothing says it really happened.

6. The sentences all deal with historical facts.

The lessons and activities included in *Close Reading with Text-Dependent Questions* meet the following Common Core State Standards for grade 4. (©Copyright 2010. National Governors Association Center for Best Practices and Council of Chief State School Officers. All rights reserved.)

The code for each standard covered in this resource is listed in the table below and on page 96. The codes are listed in boldface, and the unit numbers of the activities that meet that standard are listed in regular type. For more information about the Common Core State Standards and for a full listing of the descriptions associated with each code, go to *http://www.corestandards.org/* or visit *http://www.teachercreated.com/standards/*.

Here is an example of an English Language Arts (ELA) code and how to read it:

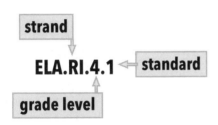

ELA Strands

L = Language
W = Writing
RI = Reading: Informational Text
RL = Reading: Literature
RF = Reading: Foundational Skills
SL = Speaking and Listening

+ +

Strand Reading: Informational Text   **Substrand** Key Ideas and Details
ELA.RI.4.1: Units 1–22
ELA.RI.4.2: Units 1–22
ELA.RI.4.3: Units 1, 3, 5, 7, 9, 11, 14–15, 19–21

Strand Reading: Informational Text   **Substrand** Craft and Structure
ELA.RI.4.4: Units 1–22
ELA.RI.4.5: Units 1–22

Strand Reading: Informational Text   **Substrand** Integration of Knowledge and Ideas
ELA.RI.4.7: Units 7–8, 11–13, 15, 17, 21–22
ELA.RI.4.8: Units 1–22

Strand Reading: Informational Text   **Substrand** Range of Reading and Level of Text Complexity
ELA.RI.4.10: Units 1–22

+ +

Strand Reading: Literature   **Substrand** Key Ideas and Details
ELA.RL.4.1: Units 2, 4–6, 8, 10, 12–14, 18–20, 22
ELA.RL.4.2: Units 2, 4–6, 8, 10, 12–14, 18–20, 22
ELA.RL.4.3: Units 2, 4–6, 8, 10, 12–14, 18–20, 22

Strand Reading: Literature   **Substrand** Craft and Structure
ELA.RL.4.4: Units 2, 4–6, 8, 10, 12–14, 18–20, 22
ELA.RL.4.5: Units 5, 8

Strand Reading: Literature   **Substrand** Range of Reading and Level of Text Complexity
ELA.RL.4.10: Units 2, 4–6, 8, 10, 12–14, 18–20, 22

+ +

Strand Reading: Foundational Skills
ELA.RF.4.3: Units 1–22

Substrand Phonics and Word Recognition

Strand Reading: Foundational Skills
ELA.RF.4.4: Units 1–22

Substrand Fluency

+ +

Strand Speaking and Listening
ELA.SL.4.1: Units 1–22
ELA.SL.4.3: Units 15, 17, 21–22

Substrand Comprehension and Collaboration

Strand Speaking and Listening
ELA.SL.4.4: Units 4, 15, 17, 21–22
ELA.SL.4.6: Units 21–22

Substrand Presentation of Knowledge and Ideas

+ +

Strand Writing
ELA.W.4.1: Units 1–20
ELA.W.4.2: Units 1–20
ELA.W.4.3: Units 2–3, 5, 8, 11, 13–14, 20

Substrand Text Types and Purposes

Strand Writing
ELA.W.4.4: Units 1–20

Substrand Production and Distribution of Writing

Strand Writing
ELA.W.4.7: Units 1–20
ELA.W.4.8: Units 1–20
ELA.W.4.9: Units 1–20

Substrand Research to Build and Present Knowledge

Strand Writing
ELA.W.4.10: Units 1–20

Substrand Range of Writing

+ +

Strand Language
ELA.L.4.1: Units 1–22
ELA.L.4.2: Units 1–22

Substrand Conventions of Standard English

Strand Language
ELA.L.4.3: Units 1–22

Substrand Knowledge of Language

Strand Language
ELA.L.4.4: Units 1–22
ELA.L.4.5: Units 1–22
ELA.L.4.6: Units 1–22

Substrand Vocabulary Acquisition and Use